ATTITUDES TOWARDS CRIME AND PUNISHMENT IN UPPER CANADA,

1830-1850: A DOCUMENTARY STUDY

J.M. Beattie

with the assistance of L.M. Distad

Working Paper of the
CENTRE OF CRIMINOLOGY
University of Toronto

1977

TABLE OF CONTENTS

PREFACE

The documents included in this volume come mainly from newspapers and the Journals of the House of Assembly of Upper Canada and of the Provincial Assembly. Almost all relate to Upper Canada directly, though several extracts from the Montreal newspaper, The Pilot, have been included either because they reprint and comment on articles in Upper Canadian newspapers or, more simply, because they provide revealing examples of attitudes widely shared in Upper Canada. The documents have been arranged around several broad themes to illustrate opinion about the causes of crime and the effectiveness of various punishments. But they are designed in particular to illuminate the reasons for a striking departure in penal practice that took place in these years -- the opening of the penitentiary at Kingston in 1835.

I am grateful to the Federal Ministry of the Solicitor General for a grant that supported my work: the views expressed in the Introduction are not, of course, necessarily shared by the Solicitor General of Canada. I am also grateful to Linda Distad for her skilful research assistance and to Lynn Bailey and Rita Christou, of the Centre of Criminology, for their help and support. I would also like to thank Merrill Distad for help in obtaining materials, and several friends and colleagues who were kind enough to give me advice at various stages: I am particularly grateful to Ramsay Cook, Gerald Craig, Richard Ericson, Susan Houston, Graeme Patterson and Paul Rutherford.

Toronto   J.M.B.
April 1977

I.   INTRODUCTION

Serious crime was not a problem in Canada in the 1830s and 1840s.
It was not uncommon for the criminal calendar at the assizes in Upper
Canada, for example, to be very light indeed when the court met for
its annual session in the various Districts of the Province (documents
2, 9). And in the 1840s, an average of only a hundred prisoners a
year were received into the penitentiary at Kingston. There was, it
is true, a distinct and sharp increase in commitments between 1842,
when sixty-eight prisoners were sent to Kingston, and 1845, when the
annual total rose to 156, but this peak was followed by as sharp a
decline by the end of the decade. And of those committed to the
penitentiary, more than half had been convicted of simple larceny --
thefts which did not involve breaking and entering or the threat of
violence. In fact, very few men and women were convicted of the
serious offences like rape and murder, or robbery and burglary. There
is some evidence, it must be said, of crimes being committed by gangs,
for the conditions that led to the apparent increase in property
offences in the mid-1840s seem also to have encouraged the formation
of a number of criminal alliances; and one of these, the so-called
Markham Gang, operated successfully for several years near Toronto (nos.
11, 12, 14, 15). But, in general, Upper Canada was not seriously
threatened by crime. A burglary in 1844 reminded the editor of a
Toronto newspaper of the great contrast with England, for Upper
Canada had hitherto, he thought, "enjoyed comparative safety from
those crimes which too frequently disturb the social harmony of the
old country".[1] And similarly, the occurrence of a murder or a robbery
was most often greeted with dour predictions that the peaceful character
of the community was about to be shattered. At the end of the decade,
a judge could still say that burglary was "an offence within my
recollection almost unknown in the Province" (no. 19).

But if serious offences were uncommon, that does not mean that
crime was not thought to be a serious problem in the 1830s and 1840s.
Accounts of trials appeared regularly in the newspapers and the contemporary

---

1. Toronto Star Transcript and General Advertiser, 26 October, 1844

debates in England and the United States on the central questions of penal philosophy and practice -- capital punishment, for example, and the virtues of imprisonment -- were followed and echoed in the Canadian press. One should not exaggerate the degree of public concern about crime. But there is no doubt that at least the punishment of crime -- how it should be dealt with -- was a frequent topic of public discussion. And this was principally because crime was regarded not simply as acts of theft or violence, but more broadly as one aspect of a much larger social question. Criminality, indeed, provided evidence of much deeper and more serious evils -- evils that threatened the moral and social fabric of the society, and that called for powerful measures of defence. It was this conviction that underlay a number of striking changes in the criminal law and in penal practice in Canada in this period, and if we are going to understand these changes it is well to begin with what Upper Canadians thought crime was and what caused it.

One clue is provided by the addresses of judges to the grand jury at the opening of assize sessions and by the chairmen of quarter sessions. Such 'charges' were regularly reported in the newspapers of the Province, and obviously reflect views commonly held by the propertied class about the sources and nature of criminality. The explanations that most easily sprang to the minds of such men when they commented on the cases for trial make it clear that they made a fundamental connection between crime and morality. The fact that not a single person was charged with theft at the quarter sessions or the assizes of the Western District in 1838 was evidence, for the chairman of the sessions, that the "District still maintained a healthy moral character" (no. 5); or, as the judge at the Bathurst District assizes said in similar circumstances two years later, it argued "a tranquil state of society, the prevalence of concord and good fellowship, and the pursuits of honest industry -- to the exclusion of idleness and profligacy, the sources of the far greater portion of the crimes that society has to lament" (no. 6). Moral order was the indispensable foundation and guarantor of a stable society, that is a society resting on harmonious social relationships, on a respectable working population and, at least by implication, on the natural authority of men of wealth and standing. If crime proceeded from immorality then it posed a much greater threat to society than the mere taking of property or

even the threat to life. It was evidence of a malaise of a much more
fundamental character, for it argued that some members of society did
not accept or had not been taught to accept the essential principles
on which the social order rested, and that the foundations of the
society were to that extent threatened. There is a good deal of
evidence that these implications were firmly drawn in Upper Canada in
the 1830s and 1840s.

To some extent a certain amount of crime was thought to be
inevitable in any society since man was sinful by nature and some
men had not overcome the consequences of the fall from grace. Such
men were led into crime by an innate corruption, despite the law or
society's best efforts to discourage them or despite, in some cases,
superior social advantages. Some men had "weak or perverted understandings", were "lost to all sense of moral feeling" or were
"abandoned to their own devices and to the snares of the devil"
(nos. 1, 13, 18). A few such men, however, could be expected in any
society and posed no serious threat to its stability: as the Chief
Justice said in 1848, "an occasional offence, however flagrant,
occurring in a large and populous District can never be justly
regarded as a reproach to its inhabitants; it only verifies the
certain truth of the imperfection of human nature" (no. 16). But,
as he went on to say, what was a problem, and a reproach, was "the
evil of crimes becoming so numerous as to diminish sensibly the
security of life and property", for that was a sign not of occasional
individual failure, but of widespread immorality in the community, and
a sign particularly of the failure of the community to impart to its
inhabitants the "instruction...on sound principles [that] not only
enlarges but exalts and purifies the mind, and curbs more or less
effectually the propensity to evil doings which is inherent in man"
(no. 2).

Here indeed was a cause of crime that was widely acknowledged:
the lack of education on sound, that is on religious, principles.
"For our own part", the Woodstock Herald concluded in 1845, "we
conceive that the prevalence of crime depends on other causes than
the mode or degree of punishment; and that the remedy for the evil
lies deeper than hanging, transportation or imprisonment can reach.

Let the legislator begin at the beginning, and provide means for the
moral and religious instruction of the people..." (no. 30). The
editor, it is true, went on to say that some alleviation of the
distresses of the poor might also decrease crime, but his first
explanation touched a much deeper and more widely held assumption
about the roots of criminality. Men fell into crime because they had
not learned the personal and social discipline that religion imparted
and had not learned to curb their baser instincts. This failure
proceeded from many causes and as many solutions could be suggested.
But for some men, at least, it argued the need for widespread education,
for education based on religious and moral teachings that would arm
especially the children of the poor against the temptations they
would inevitably face. Education, not the terror of capital punishment,
was society's best defence against crime, the Hamilton Journal argued
in 1848 on the occasion of a public hanging:

> ...we deplore the want of better knowledge, and
> coolly hang the sure fruits of its non-existence;
> we whine piteously over the natural wickedness of
> man, and give an exhibition fitted to render him
> more wicked, and hardened in his guilt. We think
> (but what use is thought without action?) that had
> a school been built on the spot where the last
> human being was launched from life to death, that
> a beginning for good might have been made -- a first
> exertion in the right path put forth. Had for
> every human creature strangled, a hundred little
> hearts been taught the truth of moral right and
> virtue, how very few would be to hang.[1]

Without the truth of moral right and virtue men would be unprotected against "the germ of immorality" (no. 39). They would be
contaminated by bad and destructive habits and be led inevitably to
crime. The clearest illustration of this was provided by the
corrosive effects of drink. It was already a truism in the 1830s that
intemperance was "the fruitful parent of crime" (no. 2). And as the
population grew and as social problems became more insistent, so too
did the conviction that the evils of liquor were largely to blame.
A Temperance movement of gradually enlarging influence attracted
support in the 1830s and 1840s and the taverns and dram shops and

---

1. Ottawa Citizen, 28 October, 1848 (reprinted from the Hamilton
   Journal)

other centers of lower-class life came under massive attack in newspapers and from the pulpits and, not least, from the Bench and the
grand jury rooms of the quarter sessions and assizes (no. 13). And
while the active Temperance cause never appealed to more than a
section even of the upper strata of society, its underlying assumptions
about the evil social effects of lower-class drinking were much more
widely accepted. They provided a handy explanation of any sudden
increase in crime. When the number of offences increased, one needed
to look no further than "to habits of intemperance and...the extra-
ordinary number of Licensed Taverns and Dram Shops...." That was the
view, for example, of the Grand Jury at the Midland District Assizes
in 1842 (no. 7). At the next session, however, the "criminal
calendar, to the credit of the District, [was] singularly light, there
being only two cases on the docquet presented to the Bench by the
Sheriff. This circumstance", a Kingston newspaper concluded, "shows
that at least in the Midland District, crime does not keep pace with
the rapid increase in the population" (no. 9). One wonders what
happened to the taverns and dram shops and their customers. They had
obviously not disappeared permanently, for at the quarter sessions
held in Kingston a year later the grand jurors again complained that
"idleness and drunkenness were the most prolific sources of crime"
and urged strong measures against these "growing evils" (no. 10). A
decline of crime was welcomed as evidence that reform was working; an
increase served notice that sterner measures were needed. Either way,
the central conviction remained secure.

One of the most obvious and direct routes from drinking to crime
was economic: it cost so much and was so debilitating that it could
drive men to steal in order to support themselves and their families.
Such necessity, of course, could also arise more directly from poor
work habits or from idleness, a simple unwillingness to work. Indeed
idleness and drink were frequently linked as twin and inseparable
evils, with idleness often seen as the fundamental and prior condition.
This was argued, for example, by the Chief Justice in charges to
grand juries in 1848 and 1849. He told the grand jury of the Newcastle
District that

> We are in the habit of imputing to drunkenness
> the crimes which deform society and create so
> much misery; and no doubt we say truly that
> drunkenness is, to a great extent, the direct
> cause. But yet, if we were to attribute them
> to idleness, rather than to drunkenness, we should,
> I think, reason more correctly; for in the first
> place, there are many of the worst crimes which
> can be traced to idleness, but with which drunken-
> ness has nothing to do; and in the next place we
> must consider that idleness is, generally speak-
> ing, the cause of drunkenness itself, and therefore
> fairly chargeable with the mischief that drunkenness
> creates (no. 16; and see 17).

Such assumptions about the nature of crime reflected a widespread
conviction, then, that its growth was a product, to quote the Chief
Justice again, "of two causes -- indulgence in dissipated habits --
especially in intoxication -- and the want of early moral and
religious training and discipline" (no. 20). The 'crime' that
contemporaries were mainly concerned about was crime against property.
Of course, no one could be unconcerned about murder; and the
occasional homicides provided opportunities for homilies on the
debilitating effects of vicious habits or the lack of religious
principles or man's unruly passions, delivered by judges and not
infrequently, convicted murderers (no. 22). Other violent acts --
rape, for example -- were similarly deplored. But the heart of the
criminal code was devoted to the protection of property and the men
who shaped and administered the laws and debated the causes of crime
were thinking primarily of arson and robbery, of burglary and theft
when they expressed alarm that crime was on the increase. Very
occasionally it was accepted that men might be driven to theft by
real necessity (no. 17). But that rarely entered the discussion.
Most often the blame was placed on the moral failings of the
criminal and on the environment in which large numbers of people were
growing up. The questions that convicts were asked when they entered
the penitentiary about their "lives and habits" and the circumstances
surrounding their crime clearly arose from the assumption that crime
could be blamed on intemperance, on deficiencies of education, on
parents' neglect of children, on the lack of skills or an unwillingness
to work. In 1836, for example the warden of Kingston asked incoming
prisoners about their own and their parents' drinking habits, about

their education, their religious practices, whether they had a trade
(no. 42). And when later a chaplain was appointed, he continued this
"investigation of the causes which led to the commission of crime" by
asking convicts about their lives and habits (no. 45).

The assumptions are clear. Crime was thought to flourish because
the environment was conducive to it and because a large proportion of
the working population lived in ignorance and was out of control.
What was at fault was the way of life of a whole class of people.
"Burglaries and robberies", Mr. Justice Sullivan said in 1849, "are
usually the crimes of a class utterly vicious and abandoned; and
where persons of this description are permitted to swarm, it is in
vain to expect that the crime that usually accompanies their presence
shall not be also found" (no. 19). And he went on to describe how
"wretched and squalid women" and "their attendant ruffians" swarmed
in the suburbs of Toronto and in neighbouring fields. Another
observer wrote about the hoards of children in the streets of Toronto,
"shivering in their filthy rags, begging, pilfering or stealing as
they find opportunity" (no. 36). "I know of no class in the community
poorer, or more to be pitied," he said, "than those who have lost
their character and have no means of prosecuting their lives but by a
repetition of their crimes" (no. 37). People without character were
people without ties to the respectable community, and without the
restraints that a concern for their standing in the community might
supply. Vagrants and foreigners were similarly detached from the
community and were similarly feared and distrusted, and thought to be
responsible for a large proportion of crimes against property (nos. 4,
12).

If crime was largely a product of social conditions that encouraged
men to be idle, to drink to excess, to abandon themselves to their
animal instincts and passions, what was to be done? How could society
be made more moral, more orderly and respectable? How could social
order be restored? The answer took many forms in Canada, as it did
in England and the United States, where the same conviction had
emerged in the early nineteenth century that crime arose from a
'criminal class', a class of 'vicious and abandoned' men and women
who lived beyond the power of religion or the law. Some urged

Temperance, others sabbatarianism, some thought the remedy lay with houses of industry or industrial schools for juveniles in trouble with the law;   still others urged an extension of popular education in order to elevate "the character of the industrious classes" (no. 16).[1] But these concerns for moral reform also inevitably shaped the criminal law and the punishment of crime. Indeed, the reform of the criminal came to be seen as a key to the future stability of the society;   and the conviction that such reform was possible brought striking new departures in these decades that were to shape profoundly future penal practice in the country.

* * * * * * * * *

The English criminal code introduced into Quebec after 1763 and into Upper Canada thirty years later was coming under attack in England. Its central assumptions were being increasingly challenged -- particularly the notion that the only effective means of preventing crime was to deter would-be offenders by the terror of example. Shaming and coercive punishments dominated the old penal system and were applied to crimes of all levels of seriousness. At the centre of the 'bloody code' was capital punishment: its dominating image was the gallows. By the end of the eighteenth century, indeed, some two hundred crimes -- most of them varieties of property offences -- were subject to hanging and the great umbrella of terror that this criminal code created allowed those who administered it and the gentlemen of England in whose interests and on whose behalf it was mainly run to select victims for periodic demonstrations of the power and majesty of the law. Not everyone convicted of a capital offence could have been hanged, for the bloodbath would have undermined public acceptance of the law. Selection of victims was essential, and around the discretion of judges and juries and the royal prerogative of pardon there developed in the course of the eighteenth century an elaborate system which saved large numbers from the gallows -- those convicted of relatively minor crimes, those who could bring

1. On this see Susan E. Houston, "Politics, Schools and Social Change in Upper Canada," Canadian Historical Review, vol. Llll, no. 3, Sept. 1972, pp. 249-271

testimony to their good character, those who could enlist the support
of the rich and powerful -- and left the worst offenders and the
friendless to be hanged as examples. It was a system that did a
great deal to sustain the authority of the social elite, especially
in rural society, for they had it in their hands to rid their local
community of a troublemaker or to extract deference and obedience
from those they saved. Thus, though the law was clearly illogical
and inconsistent, it had many defenders.

Not everyone, however, was complaisant, not even every gentleman
and aristocrat, for it was becoming increasingly apparent in the
second half of the eighteenth century that the law and judicial system
were not performing their main task -- to restrain crime. By the 1760s
and 1770s, reform was being urged. It was stimulated by both humani-
tarian and utilitarian considerations and was fed by many sources.
But the reformers tended to have one agreed objective -- to reduce
the scope of capital punishment, not so much because it was inhumane,
but because it was ineffective. Capital punishment, it was argued,
distorted the whole system of judicial administration. Because minor
offenders were in danger of being hanged, victims refused to prosecute
or juries refused to convict. The law was thus brought into disrepute
and crime was encouraged because criminals could be tolerably sure
that they would not suffer even if they were caught. What reformers
argued for in place of the gallows -- especially for minor crimes
against property -- were moderate, certain punishments, graded to
the seriousness of the crime and applied with uniformity to every
prisoner; and punishments that, in addition, would not simply coerce
and brutalize offenders, but that would reform them. By the last
third of the eighteenth century, imprisonment came to seem ideally
suited to perform this double task of punishing and reforming,
especially imprisonment that involved both work and religious instruction.
Before this period imprisonment was only rarely ordered as a punishment, and prisons were simply places of custody for those awaiting
trial. Conditions in them were hideous. The new conviction that
imprisonment under the right conditions would decrease crime encouraged
a considerable interest in the old gaols. John Howard's investigations
in the 1770s inspired a generation of reformers and the efforts to
reform both the prisons and the criminal law developed in parallel

thereafter. By the 1820s the new dogma had effected massive changes
in the law and the penal system. An Act of 1827 reduced the scope of
capital punishment significantly, beginning a process that would soon
remove hanging as the penalty for all but a handful of crimes. And
by the 1820s, too, reports of the success of model prisons in the
United States brought further encouragement to those who believed
that imprisonment under the proper conditions might well eliminate
the scourge of crime.

The criminal code that was introduced into Upper Canada was
thus already changing rapidly in England. Change, while not automatic,
followed soon in Canada. In 1831 a Select Committee of the House of
Assembly of Upper Canada advocated new departures in penal practice
and the building of a penitentiary because of the evident failures
of the old English criminal code that was still in force in the
province. Capital punishment was still applied in Canada to dozens and
dozens of offences. But, as the committee pointed out, the law was
almost never put into effect, "so that the law as practised at
present amounts very nearly to an act of indemnity for all minor
offences" (no. 40). Two years later, in 1833, capital punishment
was removed from large numbers of petty crimes as it had been in
England six years earlier (3 Will IV, c. 3). Some twelve offences
remained capital, including murder, rape, robbery, burglary and arson.
But in 1841 most of these were also removed from the capital list and
henceforth only murder and treason were in effect punishable on the
gallows.

The alternative punishment that made these changes possible was
imprisonment at hard labour in the penitentiary. As in England, this
presented a new departure, a new hope and new intention, in penal
practice -- to reduce crime by reforming the criminal, rather than by
terror and by public demonstrations of the power of the law. Of
course, many of the older assumptions about the function of the
law and judicial administration remained at work. The murder of a
master by his servant suggested to the mayor of Toronto the necessity
for "some prompt proceedings...which will have a tendency to strike awe

in the public mind".[1] An increase in arson in 1849 required, the
Chief Justice thought, "some terrible examples".[2] And of course
public executions remained even after 1841 to demonstrate "the
majesty of the law" (no. 23) and to prove that "justice _dares_
array herself in terrors when it is deemed necessary" (no. 41). The
hope that public displays of the "sword of justice" would deter
criminals did not disappear. And deterrence remained for many the
principal value of the new emphasis on work discipline in penal
institutions, for they thought that while hardened criminals laughed
at death, they feared being made to work (no. 33). But the conviction
that crime could only be eliminated if criminals were reformed and
if the "character of the industrious classes" were elevated became
increasingly dominant and led to opposition to public executions and
then in the 1840s to a flurry of public agitation for the total
abolition of the death penalty.

Even many of those who remained convinced that capital punishment was essential as a deterrent to murder came to oppose public
hangings, partly because they thought that the crowd provided
criminals with numerous opportunities for business, partly because
public execution made the criminal a hero with a section of the
population and drew other young men into crime (nos. 26, 27, 30).
But perhaps the main opposition -- in Canada as in England -- arose
from the general effect that executions were thought to have on the
public. The great crowds that were invariably attracted to the
"disgusting ceremony" -- on one occasion the crowd was estimated at
five or six thousand -- were thought to be "degraded in character"
by a scene that could "only serve to brutalize the mind of the populace" (nos. 22, 26, 27). Executions encouraged "moral insensibility"
and "a morbid and depraved appetite for horrors" and in general
worked against that moral uplift that reformers thought essential if
crime was to be eliminated (no. 32).

---

1. Bytown Gazette, 24 August 1843
2. British Colonist, 30 October, 1849

More fundamental was the opposition to capital punishment in
any form, an opposition that had been voiced in the 1830s, but that
became more vociferous in the middle of the next decade as crime
appeared to increase. There was heated debate in the late 1840s
in Canada, as there was in England and the United States, about
capital punishment. Some of those who wanted it entirely abolished
argued that the State had no more right than an individual to take away
life; others that a sinner should not be sent to face Divine judgement
unrepentant; it was also argued that capital punishment was forbidden
by Christianity, an argument that could be as readily supported by
passages from the Bible as the case for hanging (nos. 28, 29, 33).
But perhaps the heart of the argument against capital punishment
centered on its failure to prevent crime and its failure to improve
public morals. That was indeed for many the crucial point. At a
public meeting in Montreal in 1849 it was resolved that "the object
of all punishment ought to be the reformation of the criminal, the
repression of crime, and the protection of society" and it was clear
from the discussion that no one present thought that capital punishment advanced any of these objectives (no. 33). What they wanted was
more effective imprisonment at hard labour. This would "restrain the
criminal from doing more injury to society...[and] give him time and
means for repentance...but wait the calling the soul to God who gave
it". Crime could not be prevented by "such barbarous animal punishments"
as hanging, another speaker said, but only by fundamental changes in
the habits of the poor. "Let society", he said, "take an interest in
the welfare of the poor, the destitute, the uneducated children of
misfortune; let us establish Industrial Schools; let us establish
Houses of Industry; let us improve Prison Discipline...let us begin
to build the pyramid of social reform upon its base." Since crime
was thought to be the product of a criminal class that lived in
destitution and ignorance, that lived without the restraints of
morality and religion or the restraints that a concern for their good
character imposed on the respectable members of the society, crime
could only be prevented and society protected if the habits and
behaviour of the lower orders of the population were changed. Industrial
schools; houses of industry; prison discipline: these were to be
the instruments of reform. Internal discipline and good work habits
would succeed in protecting property from the envy of the lower orders

where the horrors of the gallows had failed. Good laws and even-
handed administration, the Grand Jury of the Home District declared
in 1845, would do much to

> uphold the purity, and elevate the character of
> the population, to call down a blessing upon the
> country; and to show the world that whilst our
> Institutions are wisely and anxiously devised for
> the full protection of the rights of property
> which the poor have the greatest temptation to
> infringe, they are with equal handed justice
> opposed to those vices which are usually considered
> to be the concomitants of wealth and luxury.[1]

* * * * * * * * *

The campaign to abolish the death penalty assumed that more
humane and more effective methods of preventing crime could be found
and that the key centered fundamentally in penal institutions in
which the poor could be taught their duty. A speaker at the Montreal
meeting was "quite certain that if they improved prison discipline,
they would very soon bring the community to the conviction that the
death penalty is a barbarous relic of the past...."

But effective prison discipline required new institutions. The
old local gaols were simply places of detention in which prisoners
were herded together indiscriminately to await trial or the execution
of their sentence. They had not been designed as places of punishment
and, although prison reformers since Howard's day had urged the
necessity of classifying and separating types of prisoners and the
advantages to be derived from making prisoners work, little had been
done in the District gaols in Upper Canada to make either possible.
In the 1830s the gaols were still too small for the effective separation
of the young and the old, or of the convicted murderer and the youthful
first offender. The Home District grand jury reported in 1836 that
in the District gaol "the want of room prevents the proper classification
of prisoners -- [and] that for the same reason no attempts are made

---

1. [Toronto] Examiner, 5 November 1845

to employ them...."[1] And an investigation into the twelve District
gaols in the same year revealed that although some separated debtors
from criminals and one made the further distinction between convicted
felons and those awaiting trial, as a general rule the gaols did not
have sufficient room to impose any effective separation of prisoners.
The Home District gaoler, contrary to the grand jury report, claimed
that his prisoners worked ten hours a day -- the men at breaking stones
and the women at washing blankets and scrubbing out the gaol. If that
was true, it was the only gaol in which any labour was required of
prisoners.[2]

The local gaols were the frequent targets of grand jurors and
reformers, for they seemed more designed to encourage crime than to
curb it. To allow children and youths to mix indiscriminately with
"the most hardened and irreclaimable criminals" was to guarantee that
if they went into prison uncorrupted, "untainted by the germ of
immorality", they would not long remain so (nos. 35, 39). Complaints
continued throughout this period that the gaols were schools of vice
-- "seminaries", as Lord Brougham was quoted as saying, "kept at the
public expense for the purpose of instructing his Majesty's subjects
in vice and immorality" -- (nos. 35-38, 40) and the force of the
argument led in time to the establishment not only of separation and
classification within the gaols, but to separate and specialized
institutions, to reformatories and industrial schools for juveniles and
minor offenders.

By the time such ideas were being mooted for the treatment of
the young, the conviction that prisoners should not be allowed to
'infect' one another with evil ideas, and that indeed imprisonment
should in any case be more than mere incarceration, had led to an even
more significant development. This was the establishment in 1835 of
an institution devoted to the idea that imprisonment should be
reformative, an institution that would combat the moral failings that
led men into crime and send them back into the world as new men. This
was Kingston penitentiary.

---

1. Statement of the Grand Jury of the Home District, with the Charge of
   the Judge, on the subject of the District Gaol, Journal of the House
   of Assembly (1836), Appendix no. 92

2. Gaol Reports, 1832-1835, Journal of the House of Assembly (1836),
   Appendix no. 117

* * * * * * * *

The argument that prisons should reform the criminal as well as merely punishing him can be traced to the prison reform movement that arose in England in the last third of the eighteenth century. It had been stimulated by several converging lines of thought -- by the investigations into the conditions of the gaols carried out by John Howard on the one hand, and, on the other, by the arguments of those who thought that the criminal law had been distorted and made ineffective by an excessive reliance on capital punishment. It was given further stimulus by the beginnings of the American Revolution in 1776, for the closing of the American colonies to transportation meant that the English gaols filled up immediately with those who would normally have been banished to America. In 1779, at the height of the American war, parliament accepted the principle that the government should build national penitentiaries. But, though penitentiary discipline was established in a number of gaols on local initiative, the central government did little to put the Act into effect. The expense was a considerable discouragement and other temporary sub-stitutes adopted in 1776 -- the prison ships or hulks -- continued to be relied on. It was not until 1816 that a national penitentiary was finally opened at Millbank. By the time it was fully operative in the early 1820s, new ideas and new influences deriving from prison experiments being conducted in the United States, were sweeping the Atlantic world. They had a considerable impact in England and Europe. And it was from that same source that the idea of the penitentiary entered Canada.

The institutions in question were first established in New York and Pennsylvania in the 1820s. Their aims were similar -- to reform the convict as well as to punish him -- but their methods differed and it is a measure of just how much was expected of the penitentiary that the differences engendered fierce debate and recrimination. To some extent the differences had been inherent in prison reform pro-posals during the previous fifty years. Some men believed that convicts could only be reformed by a period of solitude long enough to encourage them to reflect upon their previous sinful life, to tame their wild passions and to enable prison authorities to instruct them in religious

and moral truths. Others were convinced that while religious
instruction was important, a convict would only become a useful
member of the community if he acquired good work habits. These
slightly divergent convictions were displayed in the Pennsylvania
system (instituted in the Philadelphia prison in 1829) and in the
New York, or Auburn, system, as it was developed in the Auburn state
prison between 1819 and 1823 and at Sing-Sing in 1825. In the
Philadelphia institution the prisoners were confined separately for
the duration of their sentence: each prisoner had his own cell and
exercise yard and he saw no one during the course of his imprisonment
except the warden and the chaplain. The prisoner might be given
work, but only such tasks as could be performed alone and in his cell.
The Auburn system also strove fervently to prevent prisoners communicating with each other. But while they slept in separate cells,
during the day they ate and worked together in silence -- the benefits
being thought to be in both the work discipline they thereby acquired
and in the returns from their work which went to support the institution.

The strengths and weaknesses of these systems were widely debated
in the United States and in Europe in the 1820s and 1830s and each had
its devoted champions. Generally speaking, however, the New York, or
congregate system was most often copied, certainly in North America:
as the idea of the penitentiary spread to other eastern and to mid-
western states, variations on the Auburn model were usually adopted.
So it was in Canada. In 1831, a Select Committee appointed by the
House of Assembly of Upper Canada to investigate "the expedience of
erecting a penitentiary" reported their "firm conviction that a
penitentiary will prove highly beneficial to the province", that
"the most eligible place" for it was Kingston, and, by implication at
least, that the best model was that provided by Auburn (no. 40).
This recommendation was contained in a number of "observations"
presented to the committee by "a gentleman whose practical knowledge
of the subject entitles his opinions to a respectful consideration"
and which they passed on. His argument in favour of building a
penitentiary in Canada rested on the evident failure of alternative
punishments to stem crime. He preferred the Auburn system, largely
because he thought it provided more of a deterrent. He would make the
penitentiary "a place which by every means not cruel and not affecting

the health of the offender shall be rendered so irksome and so terrible
that during his after life he may dread nothing so much as a repetition
of the punishment...." (no. 40). He thought the reform of the criminal
strictly subordinate to this simple ambition. This did not, however,
fully reflect the grand expectations of those who built the penitentiaries in the United States in the 1820s or those who followed
them in Canada. Of course, they too wanted to deter crime: and
because they were always sensitive to the charge that prison life was
becoming too comfortable and too attractive, prison reformers frequently
talked about deterrence. It was generally agreed that life in an
institution must always be 'less-eligible' than the life of the honest
labourer outside. But the reformation of the criminal, the moulding
of a new man, was their prime objective. And this hope and expectation
underlay the building of Kingston.

The Select Committee report of 1831, which endorsed the idea of
a penitentiary, led to the appointment of commissioners to collect
information on the penitentiaries of the United States and to make
recommendations to the Assembly as to the system best suited to the
needs of Upper Canada. The commissioners -- John Macaulay, H.C.
Thomson and Henry Smith -- laid the results of their investigations
before the House in November, 1832 (no. 41). They had visited
Philadelphia, Auburn and several other American prisons, talked to
numerous administrators and had "come to the conclusion that the Auburn
system is that which is the safer to act on in this Province", largely
because it had been tried in several states and had proved its worth
whereas the insistence in Philadelphia on total separation of the
convicts was too recent to be regarded as anything but an experiment.
It was no doubt also of some importance that "the profits resulting
from joint labor are found to be greater than those which are derived
from solitary labor." Thus the commissioners recommended that the
penitentiary to be built at Kingston follow the congregate model and
they provided the House with a plan of a building and a sketch of a
prison system based on that model. This had been drawn up at their
request by the deputy keeper of Auburn, William Powers, who also gave
them a good deal of advice about particular problems -- how to deal with
female convicts, whether labour should be employed by the keeper of
the prison or let out on contract, how meals should be conducted, how

to prevent the prisoners communicating with each other in the prison
hospital, and so on.

Kingston opened in June, 1835, under the general superintendence of
a board of five inspectors and with a warden and deputy warden
responsible for the day to day operation. It was clear from the
beginning that the central aim was to combine the punishment of the
inmates with their reformation. The Act that provided for the "maintenance and government" of the penitentiary expressed the hope that
"if many offenders convicted of crimes were ordered to solitary
imprisonment, accompanied by well-regulated labour and religious
instruction, it might be the means under Providence, not only of
deterring others from the commission of like crimes, but also of
reforming the individuals, and inuring them to habits of industry..."
(4 Will IV, c. 37 [1834]). The fact that this was taken directly
from the preamble of the first English penitentiary Act of 1779 does
not make the intention any less real. From the beginning, the warden
was required to enquire into every convict's circumstances and
character -- into their education, work experience and skills, their
religion, their parents' character, their own drinking habits, and so
on -- an investigation intended, it seems clear, to discover the
particular source and nature of the moral weakness that had brought
them to the penitentiary. And in their first report, in November
1835, the inspectors requested that provision be made for a chaplain
on the grounds that his "labours are most important to the due effect
on the convict's heart of the system of discipline enforced in the
prison" (no. 42). This was one area, indeed, in which the board
thought that they could make a significant improvement in the American
penitentiary system. They quoted with approval the report of William
Crawford, who had been sent from England to look into the new American
prisons, and who emphasized the importance of the chaplain -- indeed
his indispensable role -- if the "personal reformation" of the convict
was to be accomplished. And they urged not only that a chaplain be
appointed to Kingston, but that he be given a "salary liberal enough"
to ensure "the undivided application of his mental energies to the
moral improvement of the criminals committed to his spiritual care"
(no. 42).

A more elaborate statement of the reform theme was submitted to
the Assembly by Charles Duncombe, the radical and future rebel leader,
who reported on behalf of the Penitentiary Commissioners in 1836 after
an extensive tour through the United States during which he visited
numerous prisons and penitentiaries (no. 43). In his report he compared

> their advantages with each other as places of
> mere punishment; as places of reformation; of
> moral and intellectual improvement; enquired
> into their financial concerns; how convicts
> were confined with the most certainty and safety,
> and how employed most profitably, and at the same
> time, with the least dissatisfaction to neighbour-
> ing mechanics and laborers...

But what particularly interested him were the attempts made in
the United States to reform criminals; it was in this area that he
urged the Assembly to establish and follow sound principles.

> ...as I anticipate to render more service to
> the community in this Province by the information
> obtained with regard to the great secret of the
> reformation of convicts, than in any other
> respects, I shall give you a brief statistical
> account of the penitentiaries, state prisons, etc.
> in the States I have before mentioned; their
> prison discipline and its results upon the
> convicts, and upon the community at large as
> authority for my opinions

Not all American prisons, he discovered, had adopted the new
methods developed in New York and Pennsylvania. In several western
states he found prisons in which the labour of the convicts was farmed
to an outside contractor who supplied their clothing and food and
even their guards. The convicts worked together in chain gangs and
no effort was made to prevent the young and comparatively innocent
from associating with the experienced and hardened criminal. More-
over, they received little instruction:

> The important object of penitentiary punishment
> is here lost sight of, that of reformation;
> humiliation without debasement, and education
> and increased action of the moral and intellectual
> organs of the mind, with lessened actions and

> diminished tone of the animal passions and pro-
> pensities; here is no chaplain; no Sunday School;
> or moral instruction.[1]

Thus "the great ends of punishment" were not fulfilled -- "to
deter others from crime; to prevent the aggressor from a repetition
of his offences, and, if possible, to effect the moral reformation of
all those who become amenable to the laws".[2]

If some prisons in the United States and if the District gaols
in Canada were not yet in a position to fulfill these objectives,
there was cause for optimism in the new departures in prison management on both sides of the Atlantic.

> The experience nevertheless, of some of the
> prisons of the United States, whose discipline
> is the most exact, and where classification is
> an object of careful attention; and the growing
> experience of England, and other countries of
> Europe, where the sanguinary codes which have
> been for ages in operation, are beginning to
> yield in practice to the more rational and
> humane substitution of hard labour --
> restricted diet, solitary confinement, and
> judicious classification, afford unquestion-
> able evidence, that the energies of the law
> in the suppression of crime, are most potent
> and availing, when directed with a constant
> reference to the moral faculties of our nature;
> and when clothed with that spirit that seeks
> to restore, in order that it may safely forgive
> (no. 43).

This report has been seen simply as a harbinger of future develop-
ments, "a milestone in Canadian penological history"; and Duncombe as
a man who "stood alone as a precursor of the penal reform movement of
the 1840s".[3] But this, I think, misses the point of the penitentiary
established at Kingston in 1835. Duncombe put the case for the reform

---

1. "Report of the Commissioners on the subject of Prisons, Penitentiaries,
   etc.", Journal of the House of Assembly (1836), Appendix no. 71, p. 2
   [not included in the extract printed below, no. 43]

2. Ibid., p. 3 [not included in the extract printed below, no. 43]

3. J. Jerald Bellomo, "Upper Canadian Attitudes towards Crime and
   Punishment (1832-1851)", Ontario History, March, 1972, p. 20

of the convict more lucidly and at greater length than others, but
there is no reason to think that his views were not widely shared --
not perhaps by large numbers of people, but certainly by those who had
been working since 1830 towards the establishment of the penitentiary.
Duncombe's ideas indeed were commonplace among those who had come to
see crime as a moral disease and to accept that some new institutional
measures were required to eradicate it. We have seen this in the
first reports of the inspectors in 1835 when they argued for a full-
time chaplain. One can see it in many of the subsequent reports of
the inspectors, of the warden and of the chaplain himself, after he
was appointed in 1836, and in the rules and regulations of the penitentiary published by the board of inspectors in that same year (no.
44).

Apart from the fact that these rules specifically enjoined the
warden never to "lose sight of the reformation of the prisoners in his
charge", the system of discipline and work that was adopted, the whole
tenor and structure of the life that the penitentiary was intended to
create, indicates that its founders aimed at reforming prisoners as
well as simply punishing them for their past offences and deterring
them from future transgressions. The prison routine was very simply:
the prisoners were "kept constantly employed at hard labor during
the day time" and kept "singly in a cell at night". They were not to
be allowed to speak to or in any way communicate with each other.

> They are to labor diligently and preserve unbroken
> silence. They must not exchange a word with one
> another under any pretense whatsoever, nor communi-
> cate with one another, nor with any one else, by
> writing.
>
> They must not exchange looks, winks, laugh, nod or
> gesticulate to each other, nor shall they make use
> of any signs, except such as are necessary to ex-
> plain their wants to the waiters....
>
> They are not to stop work nor suffer their attention
> to be drawn from it. They are not to gaze at visitors
> when passing through the prison, nor sing, dance,
> whistle, run, jump, nor do any thing which may have
> the slightest tendency to disturb the harmony or to
> contravene the rules and regulations of the prison
> (no.44).

The point clearly was to impose regularity of labour and good
work habits on men who were assumed to have been lazy and idle, while
at the same time isolating each man, breaking his spirit, taming his
passions and preventing the kind of corruption that indiscriminate
intercourse among the prisoners was thought to encourage. So passion-
ately was it held that separation and isolation would work its miracles
that the prisoners were not even allowed to look at each other as
they marched to and from their cells or at meals.

> The convicts shall come out of their cells in
> regular order, and march with their faces
> inclined towards the Inspection Avenue (each
> Gallery Company) successively, to the Docks
> where they shall empty the contents of their
> night tubs, cleanse them well by rinsing them,
> then partly filling them with water, they shall
> march to the place where they shall deposit
> their tubs, in rows for the day; and each
> Company proceed in the same regular order to
> its respective shop or place of occupation,
> and commence the labor of the day.
>
> ...The mess tables shall be narrow, and the
> convicts shall be seated at one side only; so
> that never being placed face to face, they
> may have no opportunity of exchanging looks
> or signs (no. 44).

The keepers were expected to enforce these rules and regulations
by inflicting "punishment with discretion" upon convicts over whom
they had immediate direction and by reporting others to the deputy
warden. The chaplain, for his part, was given "free access to the
convicts at all times, for the purpose of imparting religious
instruction and consolation." But he was also expected to "endeavour
to convince the prisoners of the justice of their sentence, and explain
to them the advantages of amendment, and enjoin upon them strict
obedience to the rules and regulations of the Penitentiary" (no. 44).

The aim, clearly enough, was to create an environment which would
remove the convict as far as possible from the evil influences that
had led him to crime. A life of "labor, silence and strict obedience"
would certainly punish him and would also act as a more effective
deterrent than a sentence to one of the local gaols, where he would
lead a life of indolence and unhealthy dissipation. The penitentiary,

by contrast, would be unattractive but healthy. In addition, it
would send him out a better man. That was the point of the harshness
of the regime and the strictness of the rules. If men committed
crimes because they were "unsubdued in temper, and strangers to the
restraints of discipline" (to quote the first warden: no. 42), then a
regimen that tamed their wildness and imposed order on their lives
would send them back into the world able to work hard and to take
their place in a respectable community. From the beginning this was
the central intention of the new institution at Kingston. It marked
a new departure in penal practice -- to eradicate crime, not simply by
punishing and deterring offenders, but by reforming them, "reformation
being", as Warden Smith said in 1836, "the primary object to be kept
in view in the management of convicts" (no. 44).

That the grand expectations were not fulfilled is hardly sur-
prising. By 1840 the inspectors, the warden, and the chaplain were
confronted by the awkward fact of recidivism (no. 45). Various
explanations suggested themselves. The chaplain thought that
sentences were often too short: "It cannot in reason be expected that
a confinement of one year, can in the least weaken a habit which has
'grown with the convict's growth and strengthened with his strength'.
The prospect of a speedy liberation naturally checks the rise of
serious reflection, and engenders contentedness, indifference or
apathy" (no. 45). In addition, both the chaplain and the inspectors
thought that the convict at his discharge should be given rather more
than the few shillings he was then entitled to. As it was they went
out of prison as destitute as when they came in, and with every
temptation to return quickly to crime to "remunerate themselves for
their past loss of time and labor" (no. 45). The inspectors had also
come to the conclusion by 1840 that some form of probation was required
at the expiration of the sentence to prevent discharged convicts
simply falling back into their old habits.

> It is certainly much easier to restrain than to re-
> form, and however great may have been the improvements
> introduced, whether under the separate or silent
> system of prison discipline, the preservation
> of convicts from falling into bad company, and to
> guard against a return to those former evil habits,
> remains, as yet, a desideratum.

> The evil is seen and felt; but with all the
> salutary restraints now in use, added to the
> moral and religious instructions placed within
> the convict's reach during the period of his
> confinement, until a plan is devised and put
> in operation to place him in a state of pro-
> bation, under some sort of surveillance after
> his discharge, little permanent reformation
> will be effected and but little progress
> made in the prevention of crime (no. 45).

The problem of recidivism continued to trouble the prison
officers throughout the 1840s. They became more conscious, for example,
of the difficulties that faced discharged convicts who tried to find
work. The chaplain pointed out in his report for 1842 that one of the
numerous obstacles in the path of the released convict was that "no
one will employ a man who has been in the Penitentiary; and I believe
it to be in no way improbable, that some have no alternative besides
a re-commitment or starvation" (no. 47; and see nos. 48-49). At
the same time, however, the chaplain continued to believe that "the
primary object for which the institution...was especially established
[was] the reformation of the offender: and that that objective was to
some extent at least being attained (nos. 46, 47).

By the late 1840s this optimism had all but gone. The warden
had quarrelled with two of his deputies in succession and forced
their dismissal. He had quarrelled with the chaplain and the surgeon.
More to the point, the penitentiary had become the object of widespread
public discussion and the vicious system of punishment that had been
necessary to keep men silent and to stop them looking at each other
gradually became known to the public and was taken up by the newspapers. The apparent sadism of the warden and his difficulties with
his staff brought Kingston into public discussion, a discussion that
led in 1848 to the establishment of a Commission to enquire into the
operation of the penitentiary. This Commission -- the driving force
of which was George Brown, the editor of the Globe, who acted as its
secretary -- produced two reports in 1849 that shed a great deal of
light on the operation of Kingston under the wardenship of Henry Smith
and that also renewed the hope that the penitentiary could once again
become a place of reform as well as punishment.

* * * * * * * *

The troubles at Kingston Penitentiary in the 1840s arose from
two related causes: the personal conduct and behaviour of the warden,
Henry Smith (especially perhaps his difficult relations with the other
officers of the prison); and the discipline that he had apparently
found necessary to put the 'silent' system into effect.

From the opening of the penitentiary Warden Smith quarrelled
with his subordinates. The charges sustained against him by the Brown
Commission (no. 56) suggested that the questions at issue revolved
around Smith's mis-management of the penitentiary's affairs -- his
neglect of his duties as warden, for example, but even more his
failure to keep proper accounts, his peculation and his deliberate
misrepresentation in returns made to the Assembly of the financial
state of the prison, of the punishments handed out, and of the conduct
of his subordinates. In addition, he had appointed his son, Francis
Smith, as kitchen-keeper and allowed him to embezzle supplies almost
at will and to torment and harass the prisoners. It seems clear
that complaints about any of these matters from his deputy or from
other officers of the prison were simply met by counter-charges from
Smith. Thus, almost from the opening of the penitentiary Smith and
the deputy warden, William Powers, conducted a running battle in
which Smith on several occasions brought complaints against his deputy
before the board of inspectors. None was ever sustained, but clearly
Smith drove Powers to resign. He left in 1840. His successor, Edward
Utting, was appointed a year later and the same pattern was repeated.
Smith complained frequently to the board about Utting's conduct of
his office and the inspectors as frequently investigated and dismissed
the charges. Finally, by what the Brown Commission was to call false
representations to the government, Smith procured Utting's dismissal
in October 1846. In the mean time, he had quarrelled with the penitentiary surgeon, Dr. Sampson, and with the chaplain, and those
quarrels led Smith to use the political influence of another of his
sons, Henry Smith, a member of parliament, to get the terms of the
Penitentiary Act changed in such a way as to increase his own authority
and his own salary and reduce the salaries of the other officers (9 Vic.
c. 4 [1846]). This had been done without the approval or knowledge

of the board of inspectors and their subsequent resignation added to
the steadily mounting pressure for a public enquiry (no. 52).
Further reason was added when the prison surgeon, Dr. Sampson,
brought charges before the new board of inspectors against Francis
Smith, and then, when these were dismissed, he appealed in October,
1847, to the Governor General.

These quarrels and the persistent stories of corruption and mismanagement finally brought the affairs of the penitentiary into
public notice and led directly to the appointment of the commission of
enquiry. But the enquiry was as much the result of another, related
set of concerns that had also been much discussed in the 1840s -- that
is the charge that discipline was being maintained at the penitentiary
only by the most brutal and inhumane punishments. Such charges were
made in several newspapers by 1846, but they were taken up particularly
by George Brown in the Globe where, week after week the savage brutality
of the Smith regime was exposed and denounced (nos. 51, 53-55). Even
Smith's defenders came to the conclusion that an enquiry was necessary
to clear his name (no. 52). And in February, 1848, the government
appointed the commission whose two reports, presented the following
year, revealed in lavish detail the full story of Henry Smith's
wardenship and made recommendations for improvements in the penitentiary
system.

The Commission heard dozens of witnesses -- including prison
guards and convicts -- and established a long list of charges against
Henry Smith involving his corruption and general mismanagement (no. 56A).
But the heart of their investigation and of their report was contained
in the eighth charge: that the warden had pursued a "cruel, indiscriminate
and ineffective" system of punishment. They produced massive evidence
of the merciless flogging of men and women, and of children as young
as eight years old. And they documented a number of cases of men and
women who had been whipped so excessively and so frequently that they
had been goaded "into a state of insanity". Some attempt had been made
by the government in 1847 to regulate the infliction of corporal
punishment; the warden and surgeon were instructed to attend each
flogging and the surgeon was required to certify in writing that the
convict was healthy enough to bear the punishment before it was

inflicted (no. 56B). This regulation had modified the use of the
cat-o'-nine-tails and the raw-hide whip and the punishment of being
shut up in a box had been introduced partially in their stead. And
some more extensive use had been made of solitary confinement and
bread-and-water diets as punishments. But the Commission found
abundant evidence that during most of his regime Smith had relied
heavily on corporal punishment to maintain discipline. In 1846, for
example, one man had been flogged sixty times in the course of the
year, another forty-eight times, and thirteen others twenty times or
more. And they found men who had been frequently "flogged with the
raw-hide three, four, and even five times in one week." Their conclusion about the extent of corporal punishment was clear enough: the
fact that the number of punishments rose from 770 in 1843 to 2,102 in
1845, and from 3,445 in 1846 to 6,063 in the next year "shows beyond
cavil, that the system pursued has been one of the most frightful
oppression" (no. 56C).

What was worse, most of these punishments were "for offences of
the most trifling character." A number of cases were investigated to
illustrate this. Alexis Lafleur, for example, was first committed
to the penitentiary when he was eleven; he was pardoned three years
later and then committed again the following year when he was fifteen.
Within three days of his arrival he was "lacerated with the lash"
before the entire prison population. Altogether, during his first
three-year sentence he was "flogged 38 times with the raw-hide and 6
times with the cats." The warden brought evidence to show that Lafleur
was "a wild creature", but the commission concluded that "the offences
for which he has been punished have been generally, talking, laughing,
and idling..." (no. 56D). Another boy whose "offences were of the
most trifling description -- such as were to be expected from a child
of 10 or 11;...was stripped to the shirt, and publicly lashed 57
times in eight and a half months" (no. 56E). And the Commission
documented several cases of men whose behaviour suggested weakness of
mind rather than deliberate disobedience of the rules but who were
nonetheless flogged -- often against the surgeon's advice. James Brown,
for example, was subjected to a total of 1182 lashes and the commission
concluded that such "incessant and severe punishment could only make
him more reckless and stupid than before" and that it had "greatly

aggravated his predisposition to insanity" (no. 56H).

The Commission condemned this treatment of children and of those whom the surgeon had declared to be insane as barbarous and inhumane. But their overriding objection to the severe and incessant corporal punishment practiced on the whole prison population was that it had defeated the true purpose of the penitentiary.

> The exasperation which such a system could only
> produce, must have bid defiance to all hope of
> reform. To see crowds of full grown men, day after
> day, and year after year, stripped and lashed in the
> presence of four or five hundred persons, because they
> whispered to their neighbour, or lifted their eyes
> to the face of a passerby, or laughed at some passing
> occurrence, must have obliterated from the minds of
> the unhappy men all perception of moral guilt, and
> thoroughly brutalized their feelings" (no. 56C).

The Commission denied that punishment on the scale that Smith had practised it was necessary to the maintenance of order in the penitentiary and by implication at least, they accused him of sadism. This may well have been true. But it is clear that what was really on trial was the system itself, the 'silent' or 'congregate' system under which Kingston was established in 1835. The warden had been asked to create an institution in which prisoners who worked side by side all day would never directly look at each other, never communicate with each other, never exchange winks, nor nod, laugh or gesticulate; they were not to whistle or run; they were not to look at visitors. Above all, they were to remain silent. Day after day, week after week, year after year, the inmates at Kingston were supposed to shuffle along the corridors to their work every morning, their heads inclined at an angle that would prevent them looking at the man ahead, work all day at a bench without making the slightest gesture to anyone around them, shuffle to the mess hall and eat meals that were cal- culated to keep them alive without pandering to 'luxurious' tastes, again without communicating in any way with anyone. The only human voices they were supposed to hear were those of the warden and the chaplain speaking to them of their sin, of the justice of their sentence, of the road to salvation through hard work, discipline and obedience.

Of course it did not 'work'. This was the nub of the problem.

Smith had not been able to stop the convicts communicating with each
other. And in attempting to maintain an impossible discipline,
excessive punishments had inevitably been resorted to. A similar
problem had arisen at Coldbath Fields Prison in England when the
'silent' system was introduced: it was reported, for example, that
in 1836, 5138 punishments had been administered there for talking and
swearing alone.[1] Smith had indeed been brutal. But the most damning
charge against him was that he had failed to fulfill the central
purpose of the penitentiary: he had failed to break the spirits of
the inmates and had failed to impose order and discipline on their
lives. He had not been able to reform them. The chaplain (not without some personal interest) testified that "as far as Reformatory
results are concerned, the Institution has been a complete failure"
and he blamed this on the warden and the inspectors who had "totally
misunderstood" the "objects of such a prison" (charge II, part 5).

The commissioners fully agreed that the warden had failed to
realize "the benefits to be derived from the silent system" (charge
II, part 1). His failure was plain to see in what appeared to be an
alarming increase in crime in the 1840s and a very great increase in
the number of inmates in the penitentiary. The population of the
prison which had been 81 at the end of the first full year of operation,
rose to about 150 in 1838 and then held steady through 1842 (Table I).
There was then a sharp increase in each of the next three years until
by 1845 another plateau was reached around 480. The prison population
had thus tripled in three years, an increase that coincided with an
inevitable increase in the level of brutality in the prison if "the
benefits of the silent system" were to be realized. Some of the
increase perhaps derived from the addition after 1840 of prisoners from
Lower Canada, from the incarceration of military offenders, and perhaps
from the imposition by the courts of slightly longer sentences.[2] But
there was also a sharp increase in the number of civilian convicts
coming into the prison in these years, and the apparent rise in the

---

1. Sidney and Beatrice Webb, English Prisons under Local Government
   (1922, repr. 1963), p.123

2. Richard Splane, Social Welfare in Ontario, 1791-1893 (Toronto,
   1965), pp. 136-7

crime rate that this suggested encouraged growing public dismay
about the failure of the penal system. It became widely believed
from the mid-1840s that the brutalizing effects of capital punishment
and the brutalizing effects of the penitentiary had both served to
harden men's hearts and had both contributed to the rise of crime.
This was Smith's central failure. An institution that was supposed
to be the key to social order and social discipline seemed actually
to be contributing to social disorder. The Brown Commission came
firmly to the conclusion that a new beginning ought to be made --
that what was required was a more humane institution and above all a
more effective institution.

Table I

Convicts in Kingston Penitentiary

Year	Number of Civilian Convicts Received	Total Population on September 30
1835	55	55
1836	44	81
1837		123
1838		154
1839	74	148
1840	96	153
1841	55	151
1842	68	164
1843	134	256
1844	147	384
1845	156	478
1846	134	480
1847	101	468
1848	103	454

* * * * * * * * *

The changes proposed for the penitentiary by the Brown Commission
are contained in their second report (no. 57). Their aims and their
assumptions were similar to those of the men who had established
Kingston almost twenty years earlier: they believed fervently that
prisons could make men worse or they could make them better -- convicts
would be either "thrown back on their old habits, more deeply versed
than before in the mysteries of crime, or returned to society with
new feelings, industrious habits, and good resolutions for the future"

-- and that that made "the management of penal Institutions a study
of deep importance." Like their predecessors, the Commissioners
also believed that there must be a good deal to be learned from
American experience, and George Brown and another member made a tour
of prisons in seven states before they formulated their own proposals.
There was less excitement about this than there had been twenty years
earlier. Crime had not been conquered anywhere. But they found some
useful examples of what they were looking for and they returned with
their two dominant convictions reinforced.

The first was that the congregate model was still to be preferred to the separate system. Complete separation was still practiced
at the Cherry Hill Penitentiary in Philadelphia and the Canadian
visitors found a good deal to admire in it. They especially approved
of the way "it calls forth warmly the confidence and affection of
the prisoner, and gives the officers such influence over his mind,
and generally affords a good opportunity for effecting the moral
reform of the criminal...." However, they also concluded "that the
human mind cannot endure protracted imprisonment under this system;
and that with all the care of the authorities, insanity, to a fearful
extent, is to be found within the walls...."[1] Full separation could
not be admitted, but its striking success in taming unruly passions
and making convicts submissive and obedient could not be overlooked.
So the Brown Commission recommended that Kingston adopt a modified
congregate plan in which every new prisoner would be kept in solitary
up to six months before being allowed to work and eat in silent
association with others. This, they thought, would bring the best of

---

1. Not included in the extract printed below (no. 57). The commissioners
   went on to say that at Cherry Hill "The prisoners, as a class, have
   a sallow, worn-out appearance; the eyes are deeply sunk, and while
   the eyelids have a heavy, languid appearance, the eyeballs glare
   with a feverish brightness. In thought and action there is a general
   sluggishness, tending towards torpidity. To this rule there are
   exceptions, but they are not numerous; these are men who with more
   or less education exercise the mind and body by reading and labour,
   properly regulated, and who have strength and resolution to refrain
   from self-abuse; for such prisoners the discipline is well suited.
   But there is a class, and a larger one it is to be feared, who sink
   from restlessness into listlessness, from listlessness to sluggishness,
   and who soon pass from that to imbecility."

both penal worlds: the submission of the separate system with the work habits and the economic benefits of the congregate system. And on this latter point they were firmer even than their predecessors that convict labour should support the expenses of the institution. They were opposed to giving the prisoner a share of the proceeds of his work, partly because they thought that the State was "entitled to his services during the confinement awarded him for the protection of society"; and partly because they wanted to maintain "those proper barriers which distinguish the honest artisan from the convict labourer".

But how were the necessarily strict rules and regulations of the silent system to be maintained? Not by the lash and the box and the other barbarities that Smith had adopted: on this they were clear and eloquent. Vicious punishments only served to harden the convicts' hearts, increased their desire for revenge and brutalized rather than softened them. Punishments were to be mild and humane. For persistent infractions of the rules, they recommended solitary confinement or even, as a last resort, corporal punishment, administered in private. And all prisoners were to be treated equally: there would be no time off for good behaviour, no special treatment for anyone.

> ...All Convicts should as far as possible be placed
> on the footing of perfect equality; each should know
> what he has to expect, and his rights and obligations
> should be strictly defined. If he break the Prison
> rules, he should also have the quantum of punishment
> to which he becomes subject. He should not witness
> the spectacle of offences similar in enormity treated
> with different degrees of severity, unless in cases
> of frequent repetition. One of the most important
> lessons to be impressed on the Convict's mind, is the
> justice of his sentence, and the impartiality with
> which it is carried into execution. This inflexibility
> by no means implies harshness as a necessary adjunct;
> on the contrary the rules of the Prison should be
> carried out in a mild and humane spirit. In place of
> wantonly seeking to degrade the criminal below his
> present position, every means should be taken to raise
> him above it. Each attempt to elevate the individual
> will act favorably on the general mass. The Convicts
> should, as much as possible, be made to understand
> that it is not the discipline to which they are sub-
> jected in the Penitentiary that degrades them, but that
> the crime which they committed outside has degraded
> them to the Penitentiary (no. 57).

Punishments were to be milder; nor would children be subjected
to them. Much of the moral indignation that stirred in the 1840s
against the penitentiary was stimulated by the way children had been
punished for behaving in child-like ways. And the instances of brutality
against the very young uncovered by the investigation encouraged the
commissioners to recommend separate treatment for juvenile offenders
-- the establishment of houses of refuge that would combine education
and labour, that would teach them a trade and put them on the road to
becoming respectable and hard-working adults. The apparent increase
in social disorder and in juvenile crime in cities like Toronto had
already suggested to many the necessity of separate institutions to
deal with juveniles, but the Brown Commission undoubtedly gave such
proposals influential encouragement.

The commissioners also gave support to the idea that education in
the penitentiary could do much to reform convicts. A certain amount of
instruction, especially in reading, had been given by the chaplain
even in the Smith regime, but the chaplain had frequently complained
that he had no proper school-room, nor sufficient books. The Brown
Commission recommended that "common education should form a systematic
part of the moral discipline, and should occupy the whole time of at
least one teacher". They thought in terms of convicts spending "at
least one hour every second day" learning to read and write, and of
even going beyond these "ordinary studies" if the inspectors thought
it safe and useful. They recommended that "a small library, carefully
selected, consisting principally of religious books, but in part of
useful works of a general character, should be procured" (no. 57).

* * * * * * * *

Thus the Brown Commission hoped to gain by 'moral suasion' what
physical force had failed to achieve.[1] Their proposals sprang from
the humane conviction that the penitentiary system during the Smith
regime had been barbarous and cruel, as well as from the conviction

1. The principal recommendations of the Commission were embodied in a
   new Penitentiary Act in 1851, for which see Splane, Social Welfare
   in Ontario, pp. 144-45

that it had defeated rather than forwarded the ends of punishment.
And their suggestions about the separate punishment of juveniles and
their hoped-for elimination of the lash and the box can only be
regarded as improvements over what had gone before. But the purpose
of the penitentiary remained what it had been -- to create an environment in which men would be re-made. The founders of Kingston would
not have disagreed with the Commission's final summary:

> In all our proceedings and recommendations, we have
> endeavoured to keep steadily before us, that the great
> object of all penal Institutions, is the prevention of
> crime; and it has ever appeared to us that there are
> four great aims which a sound penal system should ever
> keep in view, viz.--to rescue the child of ignorance
> and vice from the almost certain destruction to which
> he hastens; to guard from contamination the venial
> offender, committed, before or after the conviction,
> for a brief space to the common Gaol; to implant
> religious and moral principles and industrious habits
> on the inmate of the Penitentiary; and to strengthen
> and encourage him in his struggles with the world
> when he is discharged from confinement.

Brown and his fellow commissioners did not initiate the 'reform'
movement. The men who built Kingston Penitentiary were 'reformers' too.
From the beginning the aim of penitentiary discipline was to eliminate
crime by dealing with its root causes, rather than by terrorizing
potential criminals into lawful behaviour by the bloody example of the
gallows. This older system of law and punishment had arisen in a
simpler and more personal society in which crime had been viewed as
arising from the weakness or sinfulness of a few individuals. By
the 1820s -- in England, the United States and in Canada -- crime,
especially crime in the cities, was rapidly becoming a more frightening
phenomenon. It had come to be seen as arising from a class of men
outside the law and untouched by moral influences who were the products
of drunken and neglectful parents, of idleness, of ignorance and of
the hundreds of taverns and grog-shops that tempted them daily. These
were not isolated individuals, but a whole class suffering from a
moral disease, a disease that they would surely pass on to others
until in time the whole working population would be infected.

To maintain social order in the face of this fundamental threat
required a change in the criminal law and in penal measures. The

example of a man being hanged could not touch this diseased population:
indeed it could only brutalize them further. What was required --
as with any infectious disease -- was the isolation and treatment of
the patient. Social order could only be re-established upon new
foundations of morality and new forms of discipline and obedience.
And this could only be achieved by new penal methods. Out of this
deep conviction came the Kingston experiment in 1835. The brutalities
that followed were a product of the optimism of its founders that they
had discovered the key to social order. That it failed to suppress
crime and required re-definition within a few years need hardly
surprise us. Indeed, the dilemma posed by the attempt to punish
and reform criminals has yet to be solved.

II. DOCUMENTS

A. THE ORIGINS AND NATURE OF CRIME

1. From the Charge of the Chief Justice to the Grand Jury of the
   Midland District (1831)

   Brockville Gazette, 11 August 1831

...the calendar is comparatively light, so much so, indeed, as
to make it a subject for congratulation, that in a District populous
as this is, and while the condition of society is still, in some
degree fluctuating, there should occur in the space of a twelve month,
so few instances of aggravated crimes....we should be indulging a very
visionary expectation, if we were to imagine that the best efforts
of humanity can ever succeed in preserving a large society of men
altogether without offence. The prevalence of good example, the
effect of moral and religious instruction, and the CERTAINTY rather
than the SEVERITY of punishment (through the prompt and vigilant
administration of justice) may so far repress outrages and disorder
as to afford, on the whole, by law.... But that we can be absolutely
guarded against the occurrence of crimes even of the worst degree; we
must not expect: although on this point, as on every other, we
should endeavour after perfection in order that we make the nearest
possible approach to it.

I say nothing of the depravity of some minds, and the unhappy
violence of some tempers. There are always found to be a few men
who, although they possess too much intelligence not to be able to
distinguish between right and wrong, have yet such weak or perverted
understandings, that they seem almost reckless of consequences whether
temporal or external, and subject themselves to all the sufferings
of punishment, and the miseries of guilt, without any motive that
to a rational mind would seem to furnish an inducement to encounter
danger and remorse which must follow crimes.

2. From John Macaulay's Charge to the Grand Jury of the Midland
    District (1832)

    Brockville Gazette, 17 May, 1832

    ...Taking the whole together, and considering the extent and
population of the district, we may fairly say that though the number
of our population have rapidly increased, and though the class of
transient residents have also increased, offenders have not multiplied
in the same degree. Hence it may be inferred that public morals are
improving.... [Intemperance] is the fruitful parent of crime, wherever
it prevails. I think I am correct in regarding the diminished
frequency of indulgence in it gratifying evidence of the improving
state of public morals.... On the education of the people will depend
the future prospects of this Province. If properly attended to, one
of its effects will be to render the duties of Grand Jurors and Courts
of Justice comparatively light, for instruction imparted on sound
principles not only enlarges but exalts and purifies the mind, and
curbs more or less effectually the propensity to evil doings which
is inherent in man.

3. "Prevalent Causes of Crime" (1835)

    Kingston Chronicle and Gazette, 5 September, 1835

    1. Deficient education, early loss of parents, and consequent
neglect.
    2. Few convicts have ever learned a regular trade; and if they
were bound to any apprenticeship, they have abandoned it before their
time had lawfully expired.
    3. School education is, with most convicts, very deficient, or
entirely wanting.
    4. Intemperance, very often the consequence of loose education,
is a most appalling source of crime.
    5. By preventing intemperance and by promoting education, we are
authorised to believe that we shall prevent crime in a considerable
degree.

4. Report on the Gore District Assizes (1836)

Kingston Chronicle and Gazette, 24 August, 1836. (reprinted
from the Hamilton Gazette)

Twelve of the Convicts found guilty at our last Assizes were
taken down to the Penitentiary in Kingston by one of our steamers on
Saturday: a good riddance to the Gore District. They were nearly to
a man, strangers in this part of the Country -- 4 or 5 men of color --
an Indian, 4 Americans, 1 Irishman and we believe one Scotch.

5. From the Charge to the General Quarter Sessions for the Western
District (1838)

Western Herald and Farmers' Magazine, 17 July, 1838

...The learned chairman...proceeded to remark upon the very
satisfactory circumstance that the Gaol did not contain a single
person charged with larceny or any crime triable by the Quarter
Sessions and that it was so at the last Assizes, which proved that
this District still maintained a healthy moral character....

6. From the Judge's Charge to the Grand Jury, Bathurst District
Assizes, 1840

Bytown Gazette, 29 October, 1840

The Calendar, I am happy to say, contains few names, and if the
absence of crime prohibited by law, be a proof of prosperity -- as it
is in one very material point -- you have the satisfaction of knowing
that you enjoy this happy exception. It argues a tranquil state of
society, the prevalence of concord and good fellowship, and the pursuits of honest industry -- to the exclusion of idleness and profligacy,
the sources of the far greater portion of the crimes that society has
to lament.

7.   Grand Jury Presentment, Midland District, 1842

   Kingston Chronicle and Gazette, 28 May, 1842

   [The Grand Jury] remarked with sorrow the number of prisoners...
within the walls of the establishment. That the increase of crime
should in some measure keep pace with the growth of our population,
is what may be expected, but the Grand Jury feel satisfied that a
great portion of the offences against the law, are generally more or
less ascribable to habits of intemperance, and that the extraordinary
number of Licensed Taverns and Dram Shops in the Town and Suburbs,
contribute in no small degree to the demoralization of the Inhabitants.

8.   Report on the Huron District Assizes, 1842

   British Colonist, 1 June 1842,

   It is with pleasure we direct the attention of our readers to
the exemplary morals of the inhabitants of the Huron District, the
assizes having just terminated without a single criminal on the
calendar. The Hon. Mr. Justice McLean, who presided, commented in a
very appropriate manner upon the strong evidence that so gratifying
an incident afforded of the general good conduct of the inhabitants,
a similar circumstance having only once occurred in another district
during a period of five years. The pleasure of the learned Judge
must have been equally participated in by the Grand Jury; charges of
guilt, with all its varying depravity, being alike repugnant to the
feelings of those who have to deliberate upon them, as to the individual
whose duty it is to award the punishment that awaits their substantiation.
It is only fifteen years that the District has been settled and now
with a numerous population, we have the pleasing spectacle of its
first Assize passing away with the sword of justice reposing in its
sheath.

9. Midland District Assizes, 1843

    Kingston Chronicle and Gazette, 10 May 1843

    The Criminal calendar, to the credit of the District, is
singularly light, there being only two cases on the docquet presented
to the Bench by the Sheriff. This circumstance shows that at least in
the Midland District, crime does not keep pace with the rapid increase
in the population.

    His Honor the Judge addressed a concise but appropriate Speech
to the Grand Jury, complimenting the District on the light condition
of the Criminal Calendar.

10. Report of the Grand Jurors of the Quarter Sessions of the Midland
    District, 1844

    Kingston Chronicle and Gazette, 13 April 1844

    As was very justly observed by the Court in its address at the
opening of the Session, 'that Idleness and Drunkenness were the most
prolific sources of crime,' the Grand Jury cannot conclude their
Report without repeating what has been so often urged by previous
Grand Juries, the absolute necessity for the establishment of a
House of Industry and correction, as the best means for correcting
these growing evils, at which the great number of idle, drunken and
disorderly persons, taken up by the Police of the Town, and committed
by the Corporation of the Town, to the Gaol, may be more effectually
punished;...besides being a receptable for such persons, what might
be considered a greater blessing, would shield them from the many
dangers and temptations their exposed situations must necessarily lead
them into.

11. Gangs

British Colonist, 6 February 1846

The spread of crime in the rural districts of this province, is becoming daily more alarming. We hear of gangs of horse thieves, of forgers, and of burglars of every description, prowling about the country in organized gangs, and the peacable inhabitants have to guard themselves and their properties against the nocturnal depredations of these banditts. -- Until within the last few years, the people of Canada could repose in security in their homes at night, without even taking the precaution of bolting their doors; and as for locking the doors of their barns and other outhouses, any one proposing it would have been laughed at. It is otherwise at the present time; and the crimes which are daily committed, (of which the public prints bear witness, as well as the proceedings before Magistrates, and the criminal courts,) show what a remarkable change has taken place, as the settlement of the country has progressively advanced.

We have been led to make these few remarks, from our having received a letter from a correspondent in Pickering, relating to some burglaries which have been committed there, and which, we are given to understand, are of frequent occurrence.

12. Letter to the Editor from Pickering, 2 February 1846

British Colonist, 6 February 1846

Sir,

Permit me, through the medium of your journal, to make a few remarks on the inefficiency of the law for detecting stolen property. For the last two weeks, scarcely a night has passed without the barn or hen-roost of some resident in their neighbourhood having been broken into, and property stolen.... For any of these things not one search warrant has been applied for, and the rascals go unpunished. The

reason is obvious. It is known that a number of vagabonds are in
this vicinity who do not work, and therefore must steal; but to which
of them to impute guilt they are at a loss to discover, and the
magistrates can only give a warrant to search the premises of the
particular individual, the party deposeth he hath suspicion of.
Now were the law here in this respect as it is in Scotland, that a
general search warrant could be issued, society would be purged of
these pests....The objections that could be made to a general search
warrant are frivolous in comparison with the good that would result
from it. No honest man whose name is above suspicion would care for
the bailiff's entering his house, and saying he had a general search
warrant to look for stolen goods; neither would a search take place
there -- although, for effect, (the same as in Scotland) they might
at first visit a few houses known to be entirely above suspicion. I
trust the press will agitate this point, and that the legislature
will amend the law in this particular, as the state of the country
loudly calls for such amendment.

                            Yours truly,

                            Anti-Pilfer

13.   From the Charge of Judge Mondelet to the Grand Jury of Montreal 1846

      The Pilot, 24 October 1846

      When we consider that education and Temperance are making such
progress, that there are few unimpressed with a firm belief in the
ultimate triumph of one and the other cause, we must not despair of a
thorough change in the condition of our society. But, gentlemen, the
sooner this is done, the better; for, should apathy be found where
energy and activity are required, we shall not merely tarry in our
courses, but inevitably retrograde. It, therefore, becomes the
bounden, the imperative duty of every member of the community to aid in
accomplishing a reform which is loudly called for. The crying abuse
which we allude to, is that springing from the innumerable places of
resort in this city, where people are allowed to indulge in their

propensities for the use of spiritous liquors. The number of taverns,
and especially of that sort which hardly admits of a correct description,
is very large, and the evil resulting from their existence, is in-
calculable. To those dens of immorality, of revelry, and debauchery,
are to be traced the midnight disturbances, the affrays, the tumults
and frightful scenes, which for some time past, have been the theme of
public animadversion, of scandal, and a source of deep affliction.
It is in those low and disorderly houses, that are daily expended the
fruits of hard labour, the earnings destined for, and necessary to a
virtuous and industrious wife and mother, and to helpless children.
There all feeling, all shame forsake man -- he becomes lost to self-
respect, he ends up by being hardened to the misfortunes of others,
in proportion as he is deaf to his own interest.

That crime and disorder are on the increase, no one can doubt;
that such a deplorable state of society should be made known, in order
that a prompt, judicious, and energetic remedy may be applied to the
evil, every well wisher of his country's good, every honest and
foreseeing individual in this community, will at once, feel and
acknowledge. Temperance has gained ground, but practically speaking,
it has yet much to achieve. There is, however, no reason for gloomy
apprehensions, if that cause continues to be ably advocated, as it
has of late been. The press has not in vain, called forth its powers:
its influence has been felt, through the medium of education, without
which, temperance can never be perfectly efficient. Such has been
the moral course, attended with a partial effect...should immorality
[especially drunkenness] continue to increase in the city, sooner or
later, its destructive effects will extend far and farther every
day, until the land becomes overspread with vice and desolation.

Besides Temperance and Education, those, twin sisters, Houses
of Refuge for juvenile delinquents and houses where the idle and the
destitute might be made to earn their livelihood are so evidently
necessary that it is to be hoped that no time will now be lost.... Now
that most enlightened men are converted to the sound doctrine of the
abolition of capital and corporal punishment, and that a course of
proper education and moral influence, even in Penitentiaries, Gaols,
Houses of Refuge, and other such like places of detention, is a more

efficient protection to the community than have ever afforded other
means directed by ignorance, prejudice, anti-christian feeling and
brutal force, philanthropists have a fair opportunity of rescuing
their fellow men from that state of degradation which inevitably
follows by enlightened action. Let them only consider for a moment,
what expenses would be saved to the country, if instead of Courts of
Justice being made a stage for the public performance and exhibition
of all that is most degrading to humanity, such scenes were hidden
from public gaze, vicious men and women redeemed, and their labour,
during a detention, tempered with moral instruction, rendered fruitful to the community!

14. The Markham Gang

[Toronto] Examiner, 29 July 1846

[The activities of this gang noticed in several] "adjoining townships within the last two or three years.... A number of thefts, in
one case of a few yards of cloth, in another of a pair of breeches,
another of a few tin pans, and one of seventy or eighty dollars
accompanied by brutal violence, have been perpetrated upon the farmers,
by persons who must have acted in concert. Great terror pervaded
the minds of the timid and those living in isolated and remote
places, on account of the frequency of these depredations, and the
apparent impossibility of detecting the offenders. Now and then a
suspected person was arrested, but, for want of sufficient proof,
discharged. At last circumstances came to light that led to the
arrest of two or three, one of whom, conscious of his guilt, and
apprehensive of its being proved, took it into his head to confess
his own crimes, and turn Queen's evidence against others. Upon the
information obtained from him a number of persons in the Townships of
Whitby, Reach and Pickering were taken up and lodged in gaol. Some
of these had been suspected before, and some had not.

In the course of the trials of these men, it became evident to
every reflecting mind that, in the anxiety which every one felt to see

the villanious gang exterminated, and all who belonged to it brought
to condign punishment, there was danger that some innocent persons
might suffer with the guilty.

It was a remarkable fact that several of those charged were the
sons of respectable farmers, while others were men with wives and
children, cultivating farms of their own, with plenty and comfort
around them! What could induce such men to commit such crimes?
That a man living with his family, and owning 200 acres of land, worth
3,000 or 4,000 dollars, should join himself to a gang of ruffians,
and go prowling about the country, at one time stealing from his
neighbour a gun, at another three or four tin pans, and then dividing
the miserable booty among half a dozen companions, with almost the
certainty of detection, sooner or later, is, we should hope, a rare
occurrence. We might use the infidel's argument against miracles,
with much greater propriety, viz., 'it is contrary to our uniform
experience.' It is true, instances have been known where individuals,
without any of the ordinary inducements to crime, have exhibited an
unconquerable propensity to commit it -- who seem to have come into
the world with a eucocthea pilferendi, that has distinguished them
through life; but that a number of persons, in the same vicinity,
should be found similarly affected -- victims of the same unhappy
idiosyncrasy, is very improbable. We must see some sufficient motive,
before we can easily believe men, circumstanced as we have described,
guilty of such crimes. At all events, it does seem to us, that when
a conspiracy of this anomalous kind is asserted to be in existence,
however desirable it may be to extinguish it, yet it is infinitely
more desirable that the persons charged should be proved, beyond all
doubt, guilty -- that when persons hitherto respectable, and in a
situation far removed from want, are charged, and when consequences
so serious (affecting not themselves entirely but a numerous kindred)
must inevitably follow a conviction. Juries, if sometimes off their
guard, should be watchful and scrupulous then; that Judges, if sometimes lax and one-sided in their interpretation of the law, and
the application of its rules, should be otherwise then; that all,
in a word, concerned in the administration of justice should take
especial care that no improper spirit actuated them, and no undue
influence or prejudice biassed them.

But it has been said by Counsel...that a spirit has prevailed
throughout the late trials far more dangerous to the best interests
of the community than anything to be apprehended from the secret
combination it was sought to break up. If you speak to a juryman (of
course, there were exceptions) of the necessity of evidence from an
unpolluted source, that placed the prisoners' guilt beyond all
question, you were met with 'Ah, but such scoundrels ought to be
punished.' But how do you know the prisoner is one of them, except
from the testimony of a man who has confessed himself the blackest of
scoundrels? 'He looks like it; I've no doubt he is one of the gang!'
Is this the kind of reasoning any one of us should like to hear from
a man who had our character, liberty, and life at his disposal?
Would we think there was much justice in being arrested, and put upon
our trial as a felon, because crime ought to be punished? -- being
condemned to be hanged, because our look was sinister?

We hope (strange as it sounds) that all those persons convicted
at the late Assizes were guilty. We should be sorry to think that any
one of those now in the Penitentiary knows that he is the victim of
individual malice, and public inattention to the rules of law and
justice....But what would be, what ought to be, our feelings if it
appeared that there were political reasons for the extra-ordinary zeal
of some of our authorities, and the leanings and one-sided views of
others? It was hinted to us more than once during the Assizes that
such was the fact -- that it was thought there was no need of being
very particular, that if the prisoners were not thieves they were, at
all events, rebels; that if not punishing public offenders, they
were crushing political opponents....It did not seem to us possible
that political feeling entered into these proceedings when we heard
one of the Magistrates who was principally concerned in them, in
frequent conversation with several of the jurymen who were to try the
prisoners, descanting upon the virtues of the informers Stutts and
Spencer...inveighing against the different persons charged, and relating
numerous little circumstances within his knowledge which tended to
establish their guilt....We greatly fear that the demon of political
hatred has again profaned the temple of justice.

The Colonist has published a supplement, in which, it is pretended,

is contained a report of the trials of the 'Markham Gang'....In the
introduction [it is asserted] 'that the present association grew out
of or rather is but a continuation for other purposes, of the associations
which were originally organized for the purposes of revolt previous
to the late rebellion. The principal families implicated in the
present gang were all also implicated in the late rebellion.'....The
cat is thus out of the bag. We have it now from one who has had
access to the highest sources of information, that our authorities
thought they had discovered a ci-devant 'association' of rebels in the
'Markham Gang'....

We shall not consume much space in proving the absurdity and
falsity of the 'origin and history' which the Colonist has published
and the Canadian of last week reiterated....Whatever were the sins of
the rebels, those of plunder and robbery were almost exclusively
charged upon the lawless gangs of Orangemen, who, under cover of
authority, traversed the country, abusing defenceless women, and
appropriating to their own use whatever of private property they could
conveniently carry off....We have no doubt some of the 'Markham Gang'
were implicated in the rebellion. And it may be that a majority of
those apprehended admitted that they were 'democratic' in their
principles, for we are told these questions were asked by the magistrates.
What the question of their guilt we are unable to perceive....[The
evidence shows that the Markham Gang] grew out of the associations
founded for the avowed purpose of suppressing revolt....

...the notorious Green,...who was the most hardened villain of the
gang, was a sergeant during the 'late rebellion'....[Colonist was wrong
to assert] that none but Canadians and Americans belonged to the gang,
for Green is an Irishman...the far greater number of their robberies
were committed upon persons, who, in the vocabulary of the Colonist and
Canadian, are radicals, i.e. rebels...the gang must be a continuation
of the Orange Association, Blazers, etc., for they exhibit the same
preference for radical property. The truth is, this notion as to the
origin and political character of these loafers, is the offspring of
some wretched Tory's diseased imagination. They were as devoid of
political principles or character, as of every other character but
that of unprincipled rogues. And all who answered that description,

whatever they might call themselves, were admitted, without question, to the mysteries of the order.

[Political considerations affected the sentences awarded]. We had hoped that the day had gone in Canada when political predilections or antipathies would be suffered to influence the administration of justice.

15. The Markham Gang

Brockville Recorder, 12 November 1846

Our readers will be pleased to hear that another of the most formidable and dangerous of this notorious gang has been brought to justice, at the late assizes for the Home District. This criminal -- the well known Henry Johnson -- was tried at the last spring Assizes for the Brock District, in company with the equally notorious Robert Burr, on a charge of felony. They were acquitted; remanded on some other charge -- and removed by habeas corpus to this district, at the last Spring Assizes, when so many of the gang were convicted. Johnson was then tried on two indictments; one for house-breaking in the day time, and the other for burglary. The jury acquitted him on the former, and could not agree on the latter, and the prisoner was consequently remanded for a new trial on the latter charge. In the interim, new charges accumulated against him. One, for stealing a horse in the Newcastle District; another, for stealing a horse of William Baker in this city; another, for having, in company of Robert Burr, broken into the shop of one George Wright, of Thornhill and stolen a quantity of boots; another, for stealing a horse of Mr. Minks, of this city; another for having, in company with others, broken into the house of an old Dutchman in Whitchurch, robbed the house, and severely beaten the old man and his daughter; and another, for having, in company with Burr, knocked a man down and robbed and beat him, on the public highway. On the three first of these charges the prisoner, Henry Johnson, was fully committed for trial; on the others, the examinations were not completed, owing to the difficulty of obtaining the attendance of the necessary witnesses. On the second and third of these charges,

Johnson was put upon his trial at the late late assizes -- convicted
on both -- and sentenced to four years' imprisonment in the penitentiary. Thus, after a successful career of crime of near nine
years' continuance, has this formidable desperado been brought to
condign punishment.

We have heard some complaining of the lightness of the punishment
inflicted upon this criminal; but it must be recollected that the
Court could only deal with him upon the offences of which he had been
convicted; and could not take into account the numerous other crimes
which were charged, but not yet legally proved, against him.

The class of crimes in which Johnson was principally engaged was
burglary and horse stealing, in the execution of which he evinced so
much skill, dexterity, and promptitude, as almost to defy detection.

His principal accomplices in these crimes, were Robert Burr,
(now in the penitentiary for life), and two or three other persons
who have not yet been arrested. We are rejoiced to find that the
recent conviction and punishment of so many of this iniquitous gang,
has had the effect of breaking up, or completely paralysing the nefarious
association. Since the last Spring Assizes, warrants have been
issued for the arrest of several others of the gang, but it was found
that they had all disappeared; having disposed of their possessions
and left the country. And although there are undoubtedly some few
still remaining, yet they are broken and intimidated, and are existing
apparently in constant apprehension and terror; and are no longer, as
heretofore, feared and dreaded by the honest and well-disposed
inhabitants of the country.

16. From the Charge of the Chief Justice to the Grand Jury of the
    Newcastle District (1848)

British Colonist 24 October 1848 (from the Cobourg Star)

I perceive, gentlemen, from the Sheriff's Calendar, that as
there were but few criminal cases to be investigated at the last
Assizes, so also on the present occasion, there are but few prisoners
awaiting their trial -- and with one exception the cases are not of
the most flatigious character....

If we could be sure, Gentlemen, that crime would never hereafter
prevail in this District, to a greater extent in proportion to the
population than it has done within the last year, we should have
abundant reason to be thankful for so good a condition of things;
and might be content that it should be perpetual. Absolute freedom
from crime it will always be idle to expect, for it is assumed on the
highest authority, that 'offences must come,' and this truth is
confirmed by the experience of the oldest and best governed countries
where the laws are always supreme, and are diligently and justly
administered; -- where civilization and religious instruction, and
moral training are carried as far as it seems to be in the power of
Governments aided by the benevolent exertions of individuals to carry
them. An occasional offence however flagrant, occurring in a large
and populous District can never be justly regarded as a reproach to
its inhabitants; it only verifies the certain truth of the imperfection of human nature. But the great evil which we may hope to
avoid is the evil of crimes becoming so numerous as to diminish
sensibly the security of life and property, and to endanger that
liberty without which there can be nothing worth enjoying. What
the law alone can do for preventing the increase of crime, must depend
on the steadiness, activity and intelligence with which it is administered, for it is a true maxim that it is not so much the severity
as the certainty of punishment, which deters offenders and makes the
law respected.

But it is on other means of prevention, more slow in their
operation, but more secure and more general in their effects, that
we must depend -- I mean, of course, the religious and moral instruction

of the people. With respect to the greater diffusion of religious
principles and feelings among us, the present state of things is
highly encouraging to those who are acquainted with the past....

Then again, the measures taken, and the means supplied, for the
education of the people in the township schools is certain to have a
most happy effect at no very distant day, in elevating the character
of the industrious classes....

We are much in the habit of imputing to drunkenness the crimes
which deform society and create so much misery; and no doubt we
say truly that drunkenness is, to a great extent, the direct cause.
But yet, if we were to attribute them to idleness, rather than to
drunkenness, we should, I think, reason more correctly; for, in the
first place, there are many of the worse crimes which can be traced
to idleness, but with which drunkenness has nothing to do; and in
the next place we must consider that idleness is, generally speaking,
the cause of drunkenness itself, and therefore fairly chargeable with
the mischief that drunkenness creates. Whatever, therefore, tends to
diminish idleness by supplying the vacant hours of the farmer and the
labourer with innocent amusement, and with pleasures superior to
riotous intemperance, must tend to secure him against the danger of
his own unruly passions; for these are sure to gather strength in
unemployed hours, if the mind has been stored with no subjects for
useful and pleasing reflection.

17. From the Charge of the Chief Justice at the Home District Assizes
     (1849)

     British Colonist, 11 May 1849

     ...For all that appears on the calendar these cases, with one
exception, may belong to that class of petty thefts for which the most
appropriate punishment would be, imprisonment for a few months, with
hard labor -- if the labor could be certainly and regularly enforced,
and could be so applied as to indemnify the public in some measure,

at least, against the charge of supporting the convict. There
may be sometimes cases, though I think they are rare, where the
offender may have been incited to theft for urgent want of
food or clothing; and in such cases the humanity of Juries, and
discretion of the Court may be safely relied on for distinguishing,
so far as can be properly done, in the spirit in which the law is to
be applied. But in most of the cases it is from idleness, and the
vices which it engenders, that such offences spring; and therefore in
general the most appropriate punishment is compulsory labor. It
may teach some of the convicts that repugnance to bodily exertion may
be conquered by habit; and they may be brought to reflect how much
more wisely they would be acting if they were in future to apply the
same degree of labor voluntarily for the honest support of themselves
and their families, while they might be enjoying at the same time
their liberty, and capable, like others, of exercising a free choice.
There will be a portion of the convicts, no doubt, and I fear the
largest portion, who being naturally lazy, and having destroyed
their strength and energy by vicious habits, are not likely to overcome their aversion to labor, and with such persons the dread of being
condemned to a round of wearisome toil in every sense unprofitable
to them, may be reasonably expected to have the effect at least in
deterring them from a repetition of their crimes; and at any rate, if
suitable arrangements can be made for employing their labor economically, the public will be in some measure compensated for the expense
of their maintenance, and perhaps even some atonement may be thus
made to society for their depreditions.

18. Pronunciation of the death sentence at the Home District Assizes
     (1849)

     The Globe, 13 October 1849

     Murder is almost the only crime which under our law, is visited
with death. Of that crime you have been convicted, without any of
these mitigating circumstances that might enable me to hold out to

you the most remote chance of mercy. You seem to have been subject to misfortune and punishment before for another crime. With some persons sufferings of this kind [imprisonment] have the effect of producing repentance, and have the effect which it is contended by Almighty God that they should have, of causing us to look back upon our past lives and to make promises of amendment for the future. With some, however, who seem to be abandoned to their own devices and to the snares of the devil, punishment and misfortune have the effect of hardening the heart and destroying all moral sense...and with respect to yourself imprisonment seems to have done you no good....It is a painful thing to me, for the first time in my life, to pronounce sentence of death in the expectation that it will be carried out....

The prisoner, was almost the only man in court unmoved by this impressive address....

19. Mr. Justice Sullivan's Charge to the Grand Jury at the Home District Assizes (1849)

British Colonist, 30 October 1849

Drunkenness is no justification or excuse, upon a charge of murder, or indeed of any other crime; for, if a man wilfully place himself in a condition in which he loses all control over himself, and all discretion, he is held in law accountable for his actions when in that state, as if he were sober.... I find by the calendar that several prisoners are confined on charge of burglary, an offence within my recollection almost unknown in the Province, but from which its exemption cannot be hoped as population increases, and vice and poverty become in consequence more abundant. Burglaries and robberies are usually the crimes of a class utterly vicious and abandoned; and where persons of this description are permitted to swarm, it is in vain to expect that the crime that usually accompanies their presence shall not be also found.

Most people who live in the suburbs of this city [Toronto] or

who have extended their walks into the fields in rear of it, must
have observed, as I have, wretched and squalid women, apparently
living without home or shelter, scantily clothed, and hovering even
in our inclement weather round fires plundered from the neighbouring
woods and fences. These have their attendant ruffians, and no means
of prolonging existence but the practice of vice of the most revolting
nature. With such beings and their associates the incitements to
crime are almost invincible. They have little left to fear from the
severity of law, and nor religious or moral sensibility to keep them
from evil. Common humanity, it seems to me, should teach us to help
those whose vices even have made their condition irretrievable by
themselves, and placed them almost without hope here of hereafter.
But if this be not a sufficient inducement for the establishment of
some public asylum in which these unfortunates may be detained and
reclaimed, I have no doubt but one will soon be found, in the occurrence
of serious crime, and in the want of safety to persons and property.

20. From the Charge of the Chief Justice at the Home District Assizes
     (1850)

     The Globe, 8 January 1850

     I can only attribute this extent of crime to the influence
either separate or combined of two causes -- indulgence in dissipated
habits -- especially in intoxication -- and the want of early moral
and religious training and discipline.... Unless the moral and
religious improvement of the people extends in proportion to their
intellectual cultivation, the increase of knowledge is but an addition
to the lever by which vice dissolves the fabric of society.

B. THE DEBATE ON CAPITAL PUNISHMENT

21. On the death sentences for Treason (1838)

Western Herald and Farmers' Magazine, 8 May 1838 (from the
Niagara Reporter)

That the...three will ultimately have their sentences commuted
for transportation, we think they can be but little doubt; and indeed
it is better so perhaps -- there may be more gained by clemency than
by a too scrupulous adherence to the demands of justice, now that the
majesty of the law has on one occasion been asserted, thereby proving
that justice dares array herself in terrors when it is deemed necessary.

...We repeat also that we approve of the extension of mercy --
and we do so on broader grounds than those of expediency or policy --
we doubt the efficacy of capital punishments altogether....

22. Execution at Hamilton (1839)

British Colonist, 6 November 1839   (From the Hamilton Journal)

[Most of crowd were] respectably attired [females] whose presence
on such an occasion would otherwise have led us to suppose that they
were as degraded in rank, as, in our opinion, they were in character,
in thus voluntarily witnessing the legally constituted but disgusting
ceremony. ...[the murderer] addressed the multitude in a short speech
in which he cautioned his hearers to avoid bad company, and exhorted
them to attend to their religious duties, the neglect of which had
brought him to his untimely end.

23. British Colonist, 19 January 1842   (From the Brantford Courier)

It is high time that the majesty of the law should be vindicated
as regards Indians and Negroes. Really the government has been too
lenient to both these classes of men in Canada; for of late years
it was found to be a sufficient reason to be an Indian or Negro to
escape the gallows, no matter what crime they may have committed;
whilst in too many instances white men were punished with all the
rigours of the law.

24. The Pilot, 5 August 1844

[Following the acquital of two girls for murdering their father
a riot ensued]. This disgraceful transaction forcibly illustrates the
brutalizing tendencies of our penal system. The people are encouraged
by the laws of their country to demand blood for blood. A crime is
committed, and they seek vengenace. It never occurs to them to compen-
sate the criminal -- to make allowance for his temptation -- to
attempt his reformation. How should it? The law which dooms him to
an ignominious death makes no account of these things. The people
are taught by the law. The wild feeling of revenge which it sanctions
is planted in their breasts. The spirit of the law passes into them.
Justice and revenge are associated in their minds, and society reaps
the bitter fruits of the lesson which it has taught. ...The case is
only one amongst multitudes which prove that it is the tendency of our
retributory penal code to harden the heart, and unchristianize the
feelings of the people.

It is rumoured that the verdict of the jury in this case was
influenced by their horror of capital punishments. ...It were well
that every juryman who entertains scruples on this subject, should
explicitly state them at the commencement of the trial, and announce
his determination not to return a verdict of guilty under the circumstances.
A few such public testimonies would produce a powerful effect.

25. [Toronto] Examiner, 19 February 1845

[Effects of public executions]. Does the public execution of
a sentence of death upon a soldier act beneficially by deterring
others from a commission of crime? In many instances public exhibitions of this kind seem to have no effect in deterring from vice, if
we may judge from the results. Some authors, of high character as
profound thinkers, have recommended that capital punishments, and
indeed all corporal punishment, should invariably be carried into
effect in private because the imagination exaggerates the terror of
the penalty, while familiarity and public eclat lessens them.

26. The Pilot, 1 May 1845

The week has been rich in brutalities; no less than three
executions have taken place since our last publication! We shall
note down a few facts connected with these horrible occurrences. When
the 'condemned sermon' was preached in the presence of Tapping, one
of the criminals, a great many people, we are told, were present, who
had been admitted by tickets from the sheriff! The murderer at his
devotions is exhibited, as a wild beast at feeding time, and a
ceremony, designed to be one of peculiar solemnity, is converted into
a common show, for the gratification of a vile curiosity! The Sheriff
who sanctions this revolting practice is unworthy of his office, and
should lose it. -- Imagine the sinner on his knees before God,
presented as a spectacle, for the amusement of an idle crowd!

Tapping was hung in the presence of five or six thousand people.
The temper of those present, and the degree in which they were
impressed on the occasion, may be inferred from the fact, that the
prisoner, who bowed several times on mounting the scaffold, was
received with loud cheers and clapping of hands, as though he had been
a favourite actor making his debut! We may well ask, what next? when
the murderer makes his final appearance amidst the hearty plaudits
of the multitude.

A correspondent of the Chronicle relates, that meeting a police-
man shortly after the execution, he made some inquiries about it.
-- Whereupon the official replied, with evident admiration, 'Sir,
he (the criminal) died like a brick!' He had evidently regarded the
whole affair with the eye of a connoisseur, and looked upon the
sufferer as a hero. So much for the fine moral effect of executions,
of which some are still fond of talking.

Another of these humanizing exhibitions has just occurred. The
very frequency of executions of late is one proof of their inefficiency
for the depression of crime.

27. British Colonist, 20 May 1845 (from the Montreal Courier)

It will be a long time before we are convinced that it is a good
thing to allow a murderer or a traitor to escape unhanged, under the
idea that he may live to repent and again become a useful member of
society; it is possible and only just possible, that a wretch, who
has coolly made up his mind to take the life of his fellow man, and
has accomplished his intention, with perhaps a hundred attendant
circumstances or horror and barbarity, may, by the grace of the
Almighty, be brought to repent of his crime, but how his repentance
can benefit society, we are at a loss to know. The Government of
Great Britain has, in its lenity and forbearance, pardoned traitors;
men who had been the instigators, if not the actual perpetrators, of
many murders in working out their treasons; but we have seen no
symptoms of their repentance. We think that there are a class of
criminals of whom an example ought to be made, but we are totally
against public executions: past experience in England shows that
these exhibitions only serve to brutalize the mind of the populace,
and rogues seem to feel a sort of pride in seeing a brother rogue
die what they call 'game'. The Americans have certainly altered
their criminal law for the better in making the executions private:
enacting that the last awful scene in the life of an atrocious
criminal shall take place within the walls of the gaol, in presence of

certain public functionaries only. We believe that this is the right
plan: we are no advocates of sanguinary punishments, but we think
that there are criminals, who, both by the law of God, and for the
welfare of their fellow men, ought to be put to death, and there is
no doubt on our minds, but that a private execution, within the
gloomy walls of a gaol, witnessed by none but the functionaries of the
law, and the criminal inmates of the prison, is a far more terrible
lesson to the offenders against society, yet at large, than a public
spectacle of punishment, which has no terrors for the wicked, and
often excites feelings of pity for the culprit in the minds of the
good.

28. British Colonist, 15 July 1845 (From the London Times [Canada
     West])

     We understand that the sentence of death passed upon Samuel
Rogers a convict in our gaol, for rape, has been commuted, by His
Excellency, into confinement at hard labour for life, in the Provincial
Penitentiary. This information is interesting, as seeming to show
that those in power are desirous to abandon recourse to capital punishments, so far as their doing so may be consistent with the security
due to society and individuals. It is well to proceed with caution in
making experiments to determine whether that mode of punishment which
spares the life of the offender, will be equally (if not more effective),
in repressing crime, compared with the long established usage of
capital punishment; but could it be made practically to appear that
in so far as respects the one grand object of restraining offenders,
there is no real necessity or advantage in upholding the ancient
system; then we should think that a great step had been made towards
the realizing of a purer spirit of Christianity, the doctrines of
which religion emphatically inculcates love to our enemies, are
abhorrent to the law of retaliation and would not cut off even the most
hardened sinner from the hope of grace and salvation by abridging the
space allowed him by the Author of his being, for repentance and recon-
ciliation. Death cannot appear the heaviest of punishments to him

who regards religion as an ingenious fable, and eternal retribution
as the device of priestcraft; yet how many among men are probably in
this sad predicament, and of all others is not the class of felons
least likely to contain many exceptions? To such the fear of human
punishment can be the only deterring motives from a violation of the
Divine law, which to them is no law until its observance has been
rendered imperative by the annexation of human penalties, and it is
according to the degree in which these are rendered sure, severe
and protracted, that they will be viewed with dread and apprehension,
but the short lived sufferings of the scaffold are the jest and scorn
of the hardened unbeliever, whose views extend not beyond the dis-
solution of his mortal existence. We should therefore rejoice to see
capital punishments abolished, or at least suspended for a season,
that it may if possible be demonstrated by the issue of such
experiment that the welfare and safety of society are not most
effectually promoted by the deliberate sacrifice of human life and by
prematurely cutting off any of our fellow creatures from coming to
the knowledge of the way of salvation in a future state of existence.

29. [Toronto] Examiner, 30 July 1845 (Reprinted in The Pilot, 9
     August 1845)

We hail the present agitation of the subject of abolition of
capital punishment, as the sure harbinger of a better state of human
society. It indicates most distinctly, that the great fountains of
human charity, which are ever most copious in the humble walks of
life, are beginning to burst through the rocks which have cooped
them up. It proves that man begins at length to appreciate justly,
the high destiny of his nature, and to feel that the purpose of his
probation on earth, is to train him for another and better state of
existence hereafter, where the things of time dwindle into insigni-
ficance, and the passions and the imperfections of his nature, shall
have passed away from the horizon of his existence, leaving one broad
unbroken sky of goodness and purity to be dimmed by no shade of sin or
sorrow. Did men but more worthily appreciate the priceless value of

that immortal principle of existence which has been bestowed on us
all, how slow should we not find them in raising their hands against
the lives of their fellowmen! How awful is the consideration of
cutting off the life of a creature destined to enter on another and
unending state of existence, in a world in which he 'shall be judged
according to the deeds done in the body, whether they be good, or
whether they be evil!' If he be unworthy the mercy of his fellowmen
is he prepared for death? If he be truly penitent and prepared, is
he unfit to live?

We would teach men the awful sacredness of the value of human
life, by perpetrating, under the sanction of law, the very crime
which we denounce and desire to eradicate! Awful delusion! and
awful have been its results! 'Thou shalt not kill' is a commandment
given to us without any special limitations, or any qualifying
reservation. Its application comes home with equal strictness of
requirement, to communities as to individuals. If not one man in
the community has the delegated privilege of disregarding this law,
neither can any number of men possess this privilege. If the individual
is forbidden to steal, or to bear false witness, or to blaspheme, or
to desecrate the sabbath, or to commit adultery, equally forbidden to
do so is the whole community of individuals. Each one participating
in the perpetration of the act is as guilty as though he perpetrated
the whole act himself. The life of a man is not divisble into fractional
parts, of which each may take away his share.

But if we pretend that the community may take away life, that is,
if we say that the Legislature, in whom is vested the whole power of
the community, has the power of enacting laws authorizing the taking
away of life, we assert that each member of society has that power in
himself, and the limitation is merely as to the occasion of the exercising
of it. In other words every man possesses authority to put a fellowman
to death, provided he can secure to concurrence of his fellow-man in
the decision. But the concurrence of a universe of men cannot make
wrong right: the concurrence of a thousand millions of men, in the
taking away of one man's life could never constitute an authority for
the act, if each individual of the whole number if forbidden to commit it
it....

It is utterly impossible that any man shall feel in himself the
same merciful, benevolent, and loving mind, which was in Jesus Christ,
and yet give his sanction to the continuance of so brutalizing a
system of punishment. We shall return to this subject at an early day.
We rejoice to observe the freedom and good spirit with which the press
in England and America have taken it up. The total abolition of the
penalty of death is close at hand.

30. On Capital Punishment

The Pilot, 9 August 1845 (from the Woodstock Herald)

A controversy has arisen on this sub[ject] between the Pilot, the
editor of which argues against the expedience of such punishment in any
case, and the Kingston News, aided by the Montreal Courier maintaining
opposite ground. The advocates for the continuation of the infliction
of capital punishment in cases of murder, seem to draw their arguments
chiefly from scripture in favour of their position....

...Inasmuch...as the right of man over the life of his fellow in
certain cases is admitted to have once existed, and as there is no
distinct withdrawal of that right other than such as is contained in
the above and similar passages, which doubtless must be taken in a
limited sense, all analogies and inferences drawn from scripture for
or against the legality of capital punishment in a scriptural sense,
will naturally lead different minds to opposite conclusions. What
ought to be the subject of consideration, therefore, for the legislator,
is the efficiency or inefficiency for the end proposed -- the lessening
of the amount of crime -- or the practice which has existed in every
age, and which still exists in every nation of the world, of exacting
life for life. Within a few years the criminal code of our country
has been greatly modified, and the doom of death has ceased to be
written against several offences which were wont to incur that penalty.
We make take the conventional crime of forgery for example. The guilt
of this crime has, of course, not changed in magnitude with the change
that has taken place in the mode of punishing it. Has its frequency

become less in proportion to the mitigation of the sentence against it?
The same question is equally applicable to other crimes which recent
legislation has denuded of their capital character; and we fear the
statistics of the prisons and penitentiaries would bear melancholy
testimony against an affirmative answer to this question. It is uni-
versally admitted that crime is fearfully on the increase. Perhaps it
would be unfair to attribute this to the amelioration of the criminal
code; but if such be the fact, as we fear it is, that fact furnishes
no argument in favour of amelioration.

But whatever be the influence of the modification of the statute
book in regard to the punishment of crime, the increasing discrepancy
between the theory and practice of criminal law must forcibly strike the
most superficial observer. In nine cases out of ten the extreme sentence
of the law is not carried into execution. Why then is this demi-Draconic
enactment allowed to remain, a mere caput mortuum, on the statute book?
It is all very well to prate poetry and sentimentalism about prerogative
of mercy. But it should be remembered that justice has prerogatives too.
The law which injoins the punishment of death must either be just or
unjust, expedient or inexpedient; and mercy except in very peculiar
cases of palliation, has no legitimate business to interfere with its
enforcement. The trial, conviction and sentence of a murderer or an
incendiary have become nothing more than a solemn mockery of justice.
Either the convict is by some legerdemain or other proved to have been
insane when he committed the crime, or some conclave of old women get
up a petition for mercy and send it to the Queen all wet with maudlin
tears, and the sentence is commuted accordingly. We repeat why not
strike the sentence of death from the statute book altogether, rather
than thus make a cat's paw of the prerogative of mercy? We believe that
in no country in the world is the arm of retributive justice more relaxed
than in the neighbouring republic. There every year produces its
hecatomb of victims at the shrine of murder; but the sentimentality
of the nation, while it can look on with indifference on a deliberate
assassin in a public bar-room, cannot bear to contemplate an execution
according to law -- thus apparently affording a strong practical proof
of the inefficiency of the comparative absence of capital punishment as
a preventative of crime.

But an equally strong argument may be adduced on the other side
from the fact that the scene of an execution is invariably a busy scene
of crime; and from the fact also that the parade with which the priest
and the press usher the penitent victim up the steps of the scaffold,
as if by Jacob's ladder, into heaven, is pregnant with encouragement
for the surviving criminals to follow the same course that they may
reap the same reward.

In conclusion for the present, the subject is one for the legislator
more than for the divine. For our own part, we conceive that the prevalence of crime depends on other causes than the mode or degree of
punishment; and that the remedy for the evil lies deeper than hanging,
transportation or imprisonment can reach. Let the legislator begin at
the beginning, and provide means for the moral and religious instruction
of the people, as well as enact salutary laws for the alleviation of
the distresses of the poor; and he will do more to lessen the amount
of crime than he ever can by any tinkering of the criminal law.

31. Capital Punishment

The Pilot, 9 August 1845

--We have copied elsewhere articles from the Toronto Examiner
and Woodstock Herald on this very important subject to which we would
direct our readers attention. The Herald's article is temperately
written, and although he defends the existing mode of punishment, he
does so, not on the ground of its accordance with divine command, but
because he deems it the most efficient mode of lessening the amount of
crime, which he correctly says ought to be the subject of consideration
with the legislator. The Herald asks with reference to the crime of
forgery, -- 'Has its frequency become less in proportion to the
mitigation of the sentence against it'? Most decidedly it has, and one
important reason why it has become less is the greater certainty of
the conviction of criminals. The Herald says that 'crime is fearfully
on the increase.' Let us admit this, and what does it prove with
regard to Capital Punishment? Are there no causes for the increase

of crime <u>save the leniency of our criminal law</u>? We can scarcely believe that our Woodstock cotemporary is such an inattentive observer of passing events as seriously to attribute the increase of crime to the relaxation of our criminal code, indeed he himself admits in his concluding paragraph that 'the prevalence of crime depends on other causes than the mode or degree of punishment' and that 'the remedy lies deeper than hanging, transportation, or imprisonment can reach.' And we feel assured that 'the statistics of prisons and penitentiaries' would establish the fact that with regard to forgery, as well as other crimes the mitigation of the penalty has had the desired effect.

We quite agree with the <u>Herald</u> as to the importance of <u>the certainty</u> of punishment. The law ought not to remain a <u>caput mortuum</u> on the statute book. It is for that reason that we would urge upon leading politicians of all parties the necessity of abolishing punishment by death. It is worse than absurd, it is demoralizing to keep on the statute book laws which the public opinion of the age has unequivocally condemned. Our cotemporary, the Kingston <u>News</u>, has lately cited 'two instances of misplaced and we are inclined to think mischievous leniency in the treatment of murderers.' He says that in both cases the criminals were guilty of murder, and yet have escaped the extreme penalty, and he adds that the consequence of this system being carried into operation will be that individuals will have to carry arms in self defense, and that bravos will walk the streets. Now let us enquire into these cases. One of them is that of Rogers, lately convicted at London and sentenced to death, whose sentence has been commuted by the Executive to imprisonment for life in the Penitentiary. Now surely this punishment is not so lenient, so excessively mild, that our cotemporary need be under apprehension that any man will imbibe the impression that he may commit crime with impunity. No! The <u>News</u> must refer to the other case, which we cite, and which is a murder committed at St. Johns, N.B. After stating the particulars, the <u>Loyalist</u> adds: -- ' And yet this monster in human shape is tried by a <u>St. John Jury</u>, who, in spite of clear evidence adduced, and the Judge's charge, find him guilty of manslaughter! And why? Simply because some of the Jurymen -- as one of them has declared -- <u>are of opinion that capital punishment should be abolished</u>!!!'

We could scarcely have a stronger argument in favour of the
abolition of capital punishment. Here, assuming the statement true, a
murderer has been acquitted of the charge of murder because the jury
were opposed to capital punishment. We mean not to defend the conduct
of juries who thus violate their oaths, but many such cases have occurred
in England and the growing repugnance to capital punishment is such
that ere long there really will be impunity for crime, unless it is
abolished. --The case at St. Johns tells powerfully against the advocates
for capital punishment. Lord Metcalfe probably could give as correct
information as most men as to the effect of the punishment by death. We
believe that while his Lordship was in India he rarely ever permitted
the extreme penalty to be enforced, while in the Governments around him
executions were constantly taking place. And yet we have no doubt that
he is fully convinced that his system was the most beneficial to the
country.-- The abolition of capital punishment is one of the great
reforms of the age, and it will assuredly be carried ere many years in
England and in the United States. If Lord Metcalfe could succeed in
carrying it in Canada we should have the honour of setting an example
to other portions of the Empire, and there would be one bright spot in
Lord Metcalfe's administration for posterity to dwell on. There would
be something also on which his Lordship might reflect with a little
satisfaction to himself.

32. Capital Punishment

The Examiner, 6 January 1847

We take up the position that capital punishments promote the very
result they are established to avert. We have accused them of inefficacy. We now impeach them of direct mischief. It is only so far as law
can teach the sanctity of life, that it contributes to its preservation.
In what degree do public executions forward this end? Review the
operations of the whole system. Trace the influence of sanguinary
expiations upon society from the magistrate's room to the catastrophe in
front of the prison. From the commencement, how unnatural, how diseased

is the interest excited! The sense of the culprit's atrocity is, from
the first, lost in that of his peril.... Abhorrence of his deed must,
to a great extent, be neutralized by the piety, curiosity, or brutal
excitement produced by his fate. In due time the latter sentiments are
gratified. The wretch is led forth to a crowd whose very presence at
such a sense is an evidence of its moral insensibility.... With the
vast majority the eve of death is commemorated by revels.

33. Report of a Public Meeting in Favour of the Abolition of Capital
    Punishment held in Montreal

    The Pilot, 17 January 1849

[Dr. Nelson, M.P.P.] Does society derive any advantage from a
punishment of this kind? No. It is well known that where Capital
Punishments are most in use, there crime is most prevalent -- there men
are most reckless -- there the worst of crimes and atrocities are
perpetrated. The spirit of Christianity says, let the unfortunate
criminal live, -- spare his life, that he may atone to society for the
injury he has done it -- that he may have time for contrition and
repentance. Let him live too as an example to other unfortunate men
who may be led astray by their passions -- let him live that he may make
his peace with his God. But whilst the life of the criminal should be
spared, society must be protected. Let his existence be made of service
to society, and to the family whom his crime may have reduced to
destitution and poverty. There is something so singular in this
punishment of death -- something so revolting, that we can hardly
reflect on it without trembling....

Dr. Badgley said that before proposing the resolution which he
held in his hand he conceived it requisite to explain the data upon which
this and the other resolutions had been based. These data were, on the
one hand, historical facts, and on the other hand they comprised some
very valuable statistics, information which had been derived from sources
which all must admit to be the best that could be arrived at, viz.
Parliamentary Returns made to the British House of Commons.... [A]s legal

men, generally speaking, assign the reasons for which they would
continue and maintain Capital Punishment to be -- first, the maintenance of the majesty of the law; second, the punishment of the
offender; and third, that punishment shall serve as an example to
society, he might as well attempt to meet those reasons either by
arguments drawn from statistics, or else by arguments founded upon
common sense.... [He went on to argue that these statistics prove] that
crime had diminished by the substitution of secondary punishments for
the death penalty. [He moved the first resolution]. <u>Resolved</u> -- That
the object of all punishment ought to be the reformation of the criminal,
the repression of crime, and the protection of society.

Benj. Workman, Esq. in seconding the motion.... Now, he would ask,
did the death penalty afford that time, -- that faithful long-continued
repentance, -- that labour after a change of thought and disposition,
-- which is necessary to the criminal long steeped in vice, when he
was sentenced to be launched into eternity perhaps only forty-eight
hours after the words 'May the Lord have mercy on your soul!' had been
pronounced? (Cheers.) There could be no doubt that by hastening the
death of the convict, he was deprived of the time and means for repentance and reformation; in the first object named in the resolution,
therefore, Capital Punishment failed (Hear, hear).... As to the
protection of society -- the third proposition contained in the
resolution before the meeting, -- had society been protected by the
severe infliction of the death penalty? There was an old adage, 'The
dead tell no tales;' and when a man, in the act of committing a
robbery, thought he could escape detection by destroying his victim, he
would not hesitate to do it if the consequence of detection was death.
Crime was thus manifestly increased by the severity of punishment. (Hear,
hear).... Restrain the criminal from doing more injury to society,
-- shut him up, -- keep him at hard labour, -- give him time and means
for repentance, -- keep the murderer forever from society, -- but wait
the calling of the soul to God who gave it. (Loud cheers).
The resolution being put, was carried unanimously.

Dr. Gavin Russell ... The resolution which I have been called on
to propose [is] .... <u>Resolved</u> -- That the influence of Capital Punishment
is an assumption of power which does not rightfully belong to fallible

creatures; and being, therefore, founded on injustice, it must virtually defeat the object for which it was intended.

...We take it for granted that crimes arise from the activity of the animal propensities of our nature, in opposition to the dictates of our higher moral sentiments.... Capital Punishment defeats its object, because the tendency to murder and suicide arise from the perversion of the same destructive propensity; therefore the prospect of death is often an inducement to the commission of murder.... Capital Punishment defeats the object for which it was instituted, because it feeds and stimulates the propensity for murder.... Capital Punishment defeats the objects for which it was instituted because human tribunals, not being omniscient often cannot tell, even when the evidence is positive, whether the murderer stands at the bar or in the witness-box.... We have proved, that Capital Punishment is nothing but cruel, unjust and malignant treatment of the criminal. We have proved, that it has a debasing and demoralizing tendency on the community. We have proved, that instead of preventing crime it has a tendency, according to the nature of man, to multiply murders without number.... The crimes of individuals upon the community are but the natural punishments of that community for its neglect of important duties. Let society take the advice of Sheriff Coffin, delivered from this stand a few weeks ago, and that of Judge McCord to the Grand Jury, the other day. Let society take an interest in the welfare of the poor, the destitute, the uneducated children of misfortune; let us establish Industrial Schools; let us banish all barbarous animal punishments; let us begin to build the pyramid of social reform upon its base; then will society begin to learn whether it be in the training, the education, or the reformation of man that love is omnipotent, -- or 'For man is created in the image of his Creator, and God is love.' (Dr. Russell resumed his seat amidst loud cheering).

Mr. Popham then, in a short speech, moved -- 'That Capital Punishment is a cruel law, and may be safely supplanted by a more humane mode which will better secure the safety of society, and because it renders all reparations impossible in cases where the innocence or insanity of the prisoner may be subsequently established, who may thus have become the victim of the law'.... I contend [he went on to say]

...that human life would be safer, and capital crimes more likely to be checked, if hanging were abolished; and that the gallows neither represses crime, nor benefits the criminal. We are told, that the great virtue of the public execution consists in the terror which it produces on the spectators, and the consequent deterral of others from committing crime. Now gentlemen, an appeal to facts will not bear out this assertion. An appeal to facts will show that public executions have no terror at all on that class of society, upon whom terror is required. On the intelligent and moral portion of society, terror of this kind is certainly not necessary, but on them the general effect of those scenes is horror, while on the uneducated and immoral classes, the general feeling they produce is not dread, but insensitivity to pain, and indifference toward death. (Hear, hear) ...even private executions will not effect the desired object. It is a lamentable, but a well known, fact, that the majority of those for whom warning examples are necessary to deter from crime, are in most cases ignorant of the Bible and destitute of a proper conception of the doom which awaits the sinner; but I emphatically deny that death has at other times in any way sufficient terror, to deter them from crime.... But, although the criminal neither fears death nor the gallows, yet there is something which he does dread, something which he has always endeavored to avoid, namely hard work. Tell men of this class, that if they commit murder, they shall be confined to hard work for the remainder of their days, and it strikes me, we shall produce greater fear in their minds than can possibly be done by the threat of a Capital Punishment -- they can form at least, but a faint idea of the awfulness of death, but they can easily estimate the terror of hard labour. Then gentlemen...would it not be more humane, more Christianlike, more in accordance with the spirit of the age, if we adopted means to save life rather than destroy it; especially so, as experience incontestably proves, that it can be done without endangering the safety of society....

Dr. Frazer in seconding the resolution remarked that ...For himself he felt confident that many a hardened malefactor would risk his life to commit a dark deed, who would hesitate to do so with the prospect before him of a long life of solitary confinement. (Hear, hear).... The abolition of Capital Punishment would do much towards the diminution of crime, for then Judges and Juries would not be so scrupulous of convicting

individuals of whose guilt they had any doubt, knowing that in case of
their innocence afterwards appearing, justice could not be done to them.
-- The concurrence of crime with insanity, and the difficulty of distinguishing insanity, was another powerful argument in favour of abolishing
Capital Punishment. Incipient or latent insanity was frequently the
cause of crime. From the attention he had paid to the subject, he felt
convinced that if criminal insanity were better understood, Capital
Punishment would be less frequently inflicted....

Christopher Dunkin, Esq. moved that it be <u>Resolved</u> -- That justice,
expediency and the spirit of Christianity require that Capital Punishment
should be abolished, and that imprisonment under proper regulations
should be instituted in its stead.

...Suppose some one of us who had never been subjected to temptation
to commit crime, were to commit a very minor crime, would anyone tell
him that that man would not be far more guilty than the miserable,
brutalized, degraded wretch who has learned nothing but what is bad, and
who, yielding to the education of a lifetime, has committed a crime
which perhaps in the eye of the Almighty is less censorable than many
which we ourselves commit? We excuse our own vices, -- we sometimes too
much censure the crimes of others. Justice does not demand that we
should inflict the extreme penalty of the law upon any man for any
crime, for we do not know the extent of the guilt of the offender.
Human law should seek to protect society by restraining the criminal,
preventing him from repeating his crime, and inducing him to live well
hereafter.... But there were persons who said, 'Oh! but the fear of
death restrains crime.' Men when they commit crimes, more especially
that class of crimes for which the death penalty is enforced in our
community (thank God we do not hang for many crimes; it is very difficult to hang a man) are committed under the influence of brute passion.
The men who commit them are seldom under the influence of reflection;
they are carried away by the whirlwind of passion, which renders them
dead to every other consideration than the passion which urges them on.
Talk to him of a man being restrained by the fear of death, he could
tell them that when a man's passions were raised, he would not fear
death.... [T]here was another consideration a gentleman present had
remarked, that this fear of death is a natural instinct. He [Mr. D] was

willing to admit that it is, but it is an instinct which varies very
much in different men, some fear death much more than others and
unfortunately a very large proportion of the most depraved portion of
the community fear death least. The fear of death was greatly strengthened
by religious consideration, but the criminal classes have not understood
Christianity, it is not their faith, they have no knowledge of it, they
hardly have the capacity to receive it in its purity; and to expect
them to feel the fear of death is abusrd (Cheers). Mr. Dunkin concluded
by saying, that before Capital Punishment was abolished, prison discipline
must be greatly improved, and he was quite certain that if they improved
prison discipline, they would very soon bring the community to the
conviction that the death penalty is a barbarous relic of the past,
which is not enforced, and which, in such a community and day as ours,
it would be a public crime to attempt to enforce (Loud cheers).

C, THE PROBLEM OF THE LOCAL GAOLS

34. From the Report of John Macaulay, Chairman of the Midland District
Quarter Sessions, on the Midland District Gaol

Journal of the House of Assembly (1836) App. 44, pp. 3-4

The course of my inquiries respecting penitentiary institutions
having led me to observe the manifold defects which prevail in the plans
of the common gaols erected as well in Canada as in the United States,
it has been my earnest desire to devise some essential improvement,
that might hereafter be adopted in the construction of our District
Prisons -- It is important to prevent our Common Gaols from becoming
schools of vice, in which by means of the intercourse which may be
maintained among prisoners associated in large rooms or cells the elder
criminals have opportunities of contaminating the minds of the younger
and less experienced offenders. To check this spread of moral depravity, is
better than to punish for it, after its development and exhibition in
actual deeds of villainy -- and this is, perhaps, all that can be
accomplished by any improvement that is attainable in the architecture
and discipline of Common Gaols.

It is clear that the first step which should be taken by Society
for the prevention of the growth of vice is the careful and correct
education of youth, not merely by instruction, elementary or otherwise,
in profane literature, but by the unremitting inculcation of Religious
truths and impressing on the Juvenile mind the necessity and value of
self restraint. The polity of nations even the most enlightened has
not yet devoted suitable attention to this high duty, on which rests so
much of social order and happiness, as well as of individual purity of
life and manners. A wide field here expands before the labors of
Christian Philanthropists and Statesmen, which it will daily become
more imperative on them to occupy, as mankind advance in the path of
civilization and refinement because the incentives to crime are multiplied according to the increase of wealth and luxury and it cannot be
doubted, that if men are not under such circumstances carefully

impressed in their youth with a deep sense of their moral
obligations, they will sink under temptations, and indulging freely in
their vicious and criminal propensities incur the penalties of the law,
and be exposed to public disgrace and punishment. Early religious
instruction should form the basis of all schemes of national education;
without it, a people may become eminent in general literature and
intelligence, but not in morals.

35. Presentment of the Grand Jury of the Home District concerning the
    District Jail (1845)

    The Globe, 4 November 1845

The Jurors...find its condition to be as satisfactory as the means
at the disposal of the jailor enables him to keep it....

The Jurors, however, are strongly impressed with the conviction
that a more distinct classification of the prisoners is alike indispensable to the ends of justice, and to the moral condition of the inmates....
From their investigation of this subject, the Jurors are convinced that
such an admixture of the youthful offenders...with the most hardened
and irreclaimable criminals, must be productive of the most deplorable
consequences upon the former, and extinguish all hope of their future
reformation.

36. From a letter to the editor by R.A. Fyfe (1847)

    The Examiner, 24 February 1847

Dear Sir -- In my last I mentioned some facts taken from the prison
register of this city, proving the utter inefficiency of our penal
treatment to restrain crime, and the injurious effects of imprisonment
in the Toronto jail upon the wretched inmates.... Who can pass through

our streets without being struck with the number of children of both
sexes, which are running about shivering in their filthy rags, begging,
pilfering or stealing as they find opportunity!...   Drunkenness,
debauchery, and pilfering have impregnated every breath of air which they
inhale. At last they commit some offence while yet mere children, for
which they are seized, convicted and sent to the Toronto jail, where
they soon finish their education. The mere lad must there associate
with the villain grown hoary in iniquity, and the little girl has for a
companion the withered hag, who was corrupted to the very core, long
before her youthful companion was born!...   [argues for the establishment
of a bridewell and a reformatory for prostitutes and juvenile offenders]
....

I shall not at present discuss the questions, whether a better
system of classification could not be adopted in the prison as it now
stands, whether more permanent and systematic employment could not be
provided for the inmates, and whether some efficient means of instruction,
intellectual, moral and religious, might not be provided for the prisoners?
These questions I deem of unspeakable importance, in connection with the
jail of this city.... But were the Common Jail all that we should
expect it to be, still something further is required for the class of
offenders now more immediately under consideration. There must be some
place where reformatory measures could be brought more fully to bear
than can ever be the case in the best regulated Common Jail.

37.   From a letter to the editor from R.A. Fyfe (1847)

The Examiner, 10 March 1847

Dear Sir. -- From some remarks in my former communications, it
might be supposed that I was recommending a harsher mode of treatment
than is now adopted, to deter offenders from a repetition of their
crimes. I have no such design. The application of mere brute force
will never have a salutary moral effect upon the mind of the criminal.
Shaving, blistering, and bleeding have been found ineffectual to cure
the lunatic of his madness, and I see not how flogging, pickling, and

maiming can be considered as a proper specific for softening and humanizing those whom the wisest king of Israel charges with madness. In
insisting that the greatest care should be taken in the classification
of prisoners, I am only enforcing a law which every parent knows, or
ought to know. No sane father would allow, if he could prevent it,
his children to associate with those who were ten-fold more depraved
and wicked than they, nor would he compel his children to associate
only with those who were very much more advanced in years than themselves. In a word, he would, if he had any regard for the welfare of
his child, have reference to a principle of a wise classification in
selecting his companions. And why should not the City Council have
reference to the same principle in the treatment of those whom the law
has committed to their charge? So, while insisting that regular,
systematic employment should be furnished for the prisoners, I am only
attempting to enforce a law of our common humanity. It was never
designed by Him who made man, that any should be idle. Experience has
abundantly testified that an idle man 'tempts the Devil to tempt him'
-- that 'an idle brain is the Devil's workshop.' Regular employment
for prisoners is, therefore a <u>sine qua non</u>. It is essential to the
safety of the community into which the prisoners are to be thrown
when liberated.

In connection with the above, some suitable provision should be
made for the instruction of the jail inmates, both intellectual and
moral. <u>The females should be placed under the superintendence of
persons of their own sex.</u> They have facilities for influencing and
instructing those unhappy females, which men can never command, and
therefore their assistance in this matter should be secured.

Then suitable training should also be provided for the various
other classes of prisoners. All this should exist in our jail.

But there should be some further provisions made for convicts
<u>after</u> their term of imprisonment is expired....

I know of no class in the community poorer, or more to be pitied,
than those who have lost their character and have no means of prosecuting
their lives but by a repetition of their crimes. The poor unfortunate

person, who through age, or disease, is unable to procure a living,
can command the sympathy of the public: but the criminal, the victim
of the perfidious seducer, or of the abandoned wickedness of parents
or guardians, is left to starve in the streets or to obtain a wretched
living by means which set every law, both human and divine, at defiance.
I ask, ought this state of things to continue?

38. From the Charge of the Chief Justice at the Home District
     Assizes (1849)

     British Colonist, 30 October 1849

I shall be happy to receive your presentment on the state of the
district prison, which I expect to learn from you is as perfect as a
prison can be made, in which no arrangements exist for a corrective
system of confinement. Wherever I have been in the Province, I have
found the same deficiency complained of, and constant difficulties
occurring as to the disposal of convicts, for offences not so serious
as to involve a sentence to the Penitentiary. I fear that, in many
cases, our District Gaols are but nurseries for the great prison; and
I do not see how this is to be avoided, unless active employment,
correction and reformation are made to accompany the punishment of
imprisonment in the common Gaol.

39. Presentment of the gaol by the grand jury, York Assizes (1850)

     The Globe, 19 January, 1850

...The jurors regret that notwithstanding the repeated present-
ments that have been heretofore made...they should be called upon to
express their strong condemnation of the insufficient classification
of the prisoners, arising from the want of accommodation in the building,
whereby, the unthinking boy, and the young girl, as yet unhackneyed in
the ways of vice, untainted by the germ of immorality, incarcerated for

the first time and perhaps for some reckless freak, or trifling
technical offence...are associated with the old, the profligate, the
abandoned offender.

And if the presentment of a grand jury be not mere matter of form,
a mere mockery of justice, the jurors trust that the proper authorities
will look into and speedily apply a remedy to this crying evil.

D. THE ORIGINS OF KINGSTON PENITENTIARY, 1835-1849

40. Report of a Select Committee on the expediency of erecting a
Penitentiary

Journal of the House of Assembly (1831), Appendix, pp. 211-12

The Select Committee appointed to consider the expediency of
establishing a penitentiary within this Province, beg leave, in the
first place, to offer to the consideration of your honorable house the
following observations which have been voluntarily presented to the
committee by a gentleman whose practical knowledge of the subject
entitles his opinions to a respectful consideration.

'The necessity of a penitentiary in this country must be
obvious to everyone who has ever attended a court of justice in this
province, whether the penal code as at present exists is too severe
or not, it is not necessary to enquire, the fact is enough for us that
even when juries find a verdict of guilty, and judges pronounce sentence
of death in any case of less atrocity than murder, the person administering the government will not allow the law to be carried into execution,
and if he did, it is very probable that in such cases juries would
cease to convict, and judges to sentence, so that the law was practised
at present amounts very nearly to an act of indemnity for all minor
offences.

'What then remains in the hands of the Minister of Justice? Fining,
imprisoning, corporal punishment, and banishment.

'Fines for criminal offences may be looked upon as in their very
nature unjust because the statute under which they are inflicted without any reference to the means and circumstances of the offender
declares what shall be the maximum and minimum of the amount; so that
a judge may often find himself in such a situation that the smallest
sum he can inflict may be too much for the offence, as it may bring utter
ruin on the offender, or the highest too little, as from the circumstances

of the offender it may put him to little or no inconvenience and most
people would be of opinion that the remedy would be worse than the
disease, were an unlimited power of mulcting placed in the hands of
the judges.

'Imprisonment in the common gaols of the province is inexpedient
and pernicious in the extreme, as there is not a sufficient classification
or separation of the prisoners, so that a lad who is confined for a
simple assault, (a crime in which as there is but little moral turpitude
argues no depravity in the offender) or even on suspicion of crimes, of
that description and degree may be kept for twelve months in company
with murderers, thieves, robbers and burglars, and the most depraved
characters in the province, and a man must know but little of human
nature indeed who can for a moment suppose that such 'evil communications
will not corrupt good manners,' and that he will come out of gaol,
whether he has been guilty of the crime which brought him there or not,
a better or a wiser man then he went in. Gaols managed as most of ours
are, as Lord Brougham well remarks, are seminaries kept at the public
expense for the purpose of instructing his Majesty's subjects in vice
and immorality, and for the propagation and increase of crime.

'I am happy to have it my power to mention one instance of the
contrary of this. The gaol of the Western district, from the benevolence
and piety of the gaoler, answers all the purposes of a penitentiary as
well as a gaol possibly can do; but it would be absurd to argue from
this that the same could be done in every gaol in the province, as I
question whether it contains within its limits another man, who from
sound judgment and goodness of heart was equally capable and who would
undertake the office.

'Corporal punishment has been by many deemed improper as being
degrading. As every school-boy is flogged some time or other, all mankind who have learned to read must be degraded, according to this
argument, the tender age of the boy makes no difference, he feels an
insult more keenly than a man, and I can see no reason why, if the fear
of bodily pain is the chief inducement to learning to read Virgil and
Homer, it should not be employed to deter from crime; but I would only
employ it when it could not degrade. I would limit it to cases of

great atrocity and in their nature infamous.

'Banishing the province is so nonsensical that nothing need be
said on the subject, it is no punishment to a rogue to order him to
live on the right bank of the Niagara river instead of the left and it
is cruelly unjust to our neighbours to send among them thieves, robbers,
and burglars, to exercise their iniquitous callings in a country, where,
not being known, they cannot be guarded against.

'To penitentiaries, then, we must resort for the punishment of
crime and I shall first state what in my opinion a penitentiary ought
to be, and then answer such objections as are commonly urged against
it.

'A Penitentiary, as its name imports, should be a place to lead a
man to repent of his sins and amend his life, and if it has that
effect, so much the better, as the cause of religion gains by it, but
it is quite enough for the purposes of the public if the punishment is
so terrible that the dread of a repetition of it deters him from crime,
or his description of it, others. It should therefore be a place which
by every means not cruel and not affecting the health of the offender
shall be rendered so irksome and so terrible that during his after
life he may dread nothing so much as a repetition of the punishment,
and, if possible, that he should prefer death to such a contingency.
This can all be done by hard labor and privations and not only without
expense to the province, but possibly bringing it a revenue.

'There are many institutions of this kind in other countries that
may serve as a model for ours, but the two that I would call your
attention to and that are the best I have examined are the Bridewell
of Glasgow, and the States prison at Auburn; their discipline is something different, but they agree in the great essentials -- solitary
confinement, when not at work, silence, hard labour, privation of all
superfluities, and maintaining themselves by their own funds. I shall
briefly state the leading points of their discipline and mention to
which I give the preference. In Auburn they are fed on three meals a
day, the first consisting of what they call coffee from burned beans,
and bread, the dinner of meat, and soup, with bread and vegetables,

without milk; dinner, a soup composed of vegetables, and no meat; and
supper, I think the same as breakfast; in certain days they are allowed
a little cheese, and on Sundays a small portion of meat in their soup.
Of these I prefer the Glasgow plan because they give enough to support
life in health, and that the food is unpalatable, adds to the punishment which is just what was required. It has been objected to this,
that if you don't feed men well they cannot work so hard, consequently
cannot make so much money. The answer to this is, that a penitentiary
is for the punishment of crime, not a manufactory or a source of revenue,
or so only incidentally; for if it is necessary for punishment to
resort to solitary confinement, you must support the culprit and get no
work whatever from him, and nobody would argue against supporting
discipline in this manner because the state lost a certain number of
shillings and pence thereby.

'In Auburn silence and incessant labor are obtained by the very
simple expedient of a board skreen at the back of the workshops, with
holes bored in it, so that a man never knows whether one of the officers
of the prison may not be standing within a yard of him, looking at him
and listening to him. In Glasgow silence is compelled by a machine set
a going by a tread mill, which makes such a tremendous racket that no
conversation can be carried on, in as much as so far from hearing what
his neighbour say, a man cannot hear himself speak. I prefer the
Auburn mode as being more simple and as efficacious.

'In Glasgow there are, I believe, tasks -- in Auburn, none; a
man must work his whole time, and be punished if he does it negligently;
the latter is the most disagreeable, therefore the best.

'In Glasgow the surplus of their earnings is given to them on their
leaving the prison, on the plea that if you turn them out pennyless
you give them a strong temptation to recommence their career of iniquity.
In Auburn the whole goes to the state -- I would prefer a medium,
given them as much as will support them for some days, and carry them to
such a distance as they may not be known, where they may earn their
living by the trade they may have learned during their confinement.

'In Glasgow, I believe, they give moral and religious instruction

and education to such as require it, particularly Juvenile delinquents.
In Auburn they confine it to a sermon on Sunday. I prefer the latter
mode.

'A Penitentiary is not a school for education, if that be done at
all, it should be done in a house of refuge, when their punishment is
at an end.

'It has been objected to penitentiaries, that they do not reform
the people who are sent to them; this is acknowledged by the people
of Glasgow, and scarcely denied by those of New-York; but punishment
is meant to deter, not to reform, as any indictment will inform you;
or if reform is contemplated, it is only a secondary intention.

'It is enough that you inflict a punishment to which humanity
cannot object, and that you gain all the advantage of example without
bloodshed, and if you make the culprit no better, you certainly make
him no worse, which can't be said of confinement as practised at
present.

'The last objection I shall mention is the one which has arisen in
New York, and is coming hither; viz. that the state being able to manu-
facture cheaper, and therefore it will injure the manufacturer's
interests; an interest which, though I believe I know as much of this
country as any man in it, I have never yet been able to fall in with.

'This is exclusively an agricultural country, and we have in the
mother country, and the West Indies, a market for agricultural produce,
which it will be long before we can affect, much less supply; what
flour we send to England would not furnish each of His Majesty's
subjects within the realm, a single meal; therefore we require to
foster no manufacturing interest to consume our produce, and so long
as the farmer can get as much for his wheat as he does, and find no
difficulty in disposing of all he can raise, it can be no objection
with him that by any means he gets all his manufactured goods at half
price he at present pays.'

The objection referred to in the latter part of the foregoing

letter, is of recent origin; and should your honourable house deem it
sufficiently weighty to induce you to postpone the commencement of a
Penitentiary for another year, the committee would respectfully recommend
that a bill be passed appointing commissioners to collect information
on so important a subject, and at the same time to procure plans and
estimates of the expense of the contemplated building. For this
purpose a small grant of money will be necessary, and the committee
have no doubt that your honourable House will provide the sum required.

Your committee, however, are assured, by American gentlemen of the
highest respectability, that the present clamour in the United States
against States prisons has been raised by a few persons, for party and
political purposes, and that nineteen-twentieths of the people are
perfectly satisfied with the present system. With this assurance, and
the firm conviction that a penitentiary will prove highly beneficial
to the province, the committee do not hesitate to state that they are
in favor of appropriating a sum sufficient to erect the necessary
buildings immediately. The committee cannot with certainty, name the
sum that will be required; but judging from the cost of other public
edifices in the province, they are of opinion that ten thousand pounds
will be ample.

The prison can be so constructed as to admit of such additions as
the future wants of the province may require; and, therefore, it is
quite unnecessary to proceed, at first, upon a very extensive plan.
To meet this view of the subject, the committee have prepared a bill
which accompanies this report.

The committee cannot close their report without expressing their
opinion as to the most eligible place for erecting the projected
building. The town of Kingston and its vicinity present numerous
advantages.

It is well protected by an effective Garrison and extensive
fortifications -- the situation is healthy, and land can be purchased
at a moderate price. In addition to these recommendations, the
materials for building are abundant, and of the most substantial kind,
and the inexhaustible Quarries of stone, which exist in every direction

within the township of Kingston, will afford convicts that description
of employment which has been found by actual experiment to the most
useful in Institutions such as your committee recommend.

All which is most respectfully submitted.

H.C. Thomson
Chairman

41. Extracts from the Report of the Commissioners appointed...for the
purpose of obtaining Plans and Estimates of a Penitentiary to be
erected in this Province

Journal of the House of Assembly (1832-3), Appendix, pp. 26-41

To His Excellency Sir John Colborne, K.C.B., Lieutenant Governor
of the Province of Upper Canada....

The undersigned Commissioners, appointed by an Act passed at the
last Session of the Legislature, entitled "An Act granting to His
Majesty a sum of money to obtain Plans and Estimates of a Penitentiary
to be erected in this Province, and to appoint Commissioners for the
same" --

HUMBLY BEG LEAVE TO REPORT:
That in the early part of the month of June last, they proceeded
on a tour into the United States, in order to procure the Plans and
Estimates, and other information required by the Legislature. They
first visited the Penitentiary erected by the Government of the State
of New York, at Auburn, and spent some time, with great advantage, in
examining that Prison, and the system of Police and discipline which
was originally devised at that Establishment, together with the modes
of employing and punishing the Convicts there confined. From thence
they repaired to Sing-Sing, where the second great Penitentiary of the
State of New York, called the Mount Pleasant State Prison, is situated.
This Prison is of more recent construction than that of Auburn, but is

managed on the same principles. The Commissioners also inspected the
Prison built at Blackwell's Island by the Corporation of the City of
New York; and the Penitentiary of Connecticut, erected at Wethersfield, within a few miles of Hartford; and they were about to extend
their visits to similar Establishments at Boston and Philadelphia,
when the sudden and alarming progress of the Cholera obliged them to
change their plans and to return immediately home. The results of
such inquiries as they had an opportunity to make are now submitted,
and imperfect and defective though they may in many respects be, it is
yet hoped they will not be considered wholly unsatisfactory or insufficient.

On the merits of the Penitentiary system, it does not appear that
the Commissioners are called on to offer any elaborate argument or
observations. The Legislature, in the preamble of the Statute, have
fully expressed their sentiments on the subject, and left it no longer
a question for discussion whether it is expedient, for the more
effectual punishment of crime, to erect a Penitentiary within this
Province. The duties assigned the Commissioners were, to procure
Plans and Estimates for the building that it had been determined on to
erect, and to gather information respecting the best system of
management to be adopted on its completion....

...two systems of improved prison discipline have acquired
notoriety in the United States, namely, the Auburn system and the
Philidelphia system: both of them based on the grand principle of
solitary confinement, with labor, but differing considerably in its
practical application; both, however, aim not only at the beneficial
effects to be produced by the restraint of the convict, and the example
of his punishment, but also at the reformation of the delinquent, which,
especially among the junior classes, is far from being of rare occurrence....

[At the Eastern Penitentiary in Philadelphia] the discipline of
this Penitentiary is described by the Board of Inspectors in their
second Report made in the year 1830, as consisting in "solitary confinement at labor, with instruction in labor, in morals, and in religion."
The Board go on to declare their "judgment, founded on actual
experience, of the operation of solitary confinement with labor and
instruction, upon the moral and physical powers of the convicts."

"The evidence of the Physician (say they) with the concurring testimony of the warden, establish the fact, that neither insanity nor bodily infirmity has been produced by the mitigated solitude in which the prisoners are confined. Absolute solitude for years, without labor or moral or religious instruction, probably does bear too severely upon a social being like man, and were such the mode of punishment in this Institution, the Board would feel little hesitation in recommending its repeal -- as cruel, because calculated to undermine the moral and physical powers of the prisoner, and to disqualify him from earning his bread at the expiration of his sentence; as impolitic because when persisted in beyond a very limited time, it tends to harden rather than reform the offender, and while it produces great expense to the public, the prisoner in no way contributing by labor to his support."

"When a convict first arrives, he is placed in a cell and left alone, without work and without any book. His mind can only operate on itself; generally, but few hours elapse before he petitions for something to do, and for a bible. No instance has occurred in which such a petition has been delayed beyond a day, or two. If the prisoner have a trade that can be pursued in his cell, he is put to work, as a favor; as a reward for good behaviour and as a favor, a bible is allowed him. If he have no trade, or one that cannot be pursued in his cell, he is allowed to choose one that can, and he is instructed by one of the overseers, all of whom are master workmen in the trades they respectively superintend and teach. Thus work, and moral and religious books, are regarded and received as favors, and are withheld as a punishment."

"Intemperance and thoughtless folly are the parents of crime; and the walls of a prison are generally peopled by those who have seldom seriously reflected: hence, the first object of the officers of the Institution is, to turn the thoughts of the convict inwards upon himself, and to teach him how to think; in this, solitude is a powerful aid: hence this mode of punishment, bearing as it does with great severity upon the hardened and impenitent felon, is eminently calculated to break down his obdurate spirit; and when that important object of Penitentiary discipline has been gained, (and in any prison it frequently

is) and when the prisoner has once experienced the operation of the
principles of this Institution on a broken spirit and a contrite heart,
he learns, and he feels, that moral and religious reflection, relieved
by industrious occupation at his trade, comfort and support his mental
and physical powers, divest his solitary cell of all its horrors and
his punishment of much of its severity. The impression thus made,
instead of being destroyed by the sneers of ruffians, is cherished,
and fixed by the officers of the prison."

"No prisoner is seen by another after he enters the walls; when
the years of his confinement have passed, his old associates in crime
will be scattered over the earth, in prison or in the grave, and the
reformed prisoner looks forward from this Penitentiary with a hope that
he may pass his life, after the expiration of his sentence, undiscovered
by the community of convicts; and that should he find a spot where
he may earn his livelihood by honest industry, and acquire a new character,
and friends who are ignorant of his crime, there will be a probability
he may escape exposure to the new world he has formed around him, and
may not be deprived of his employment and again be driven by necessity
to crime, in order to obtain the means of his subsistence...."

The Auburn system consists briefly in this: "Absolute solitude
during the night; joint labor during the day, but without any communication with each other by word or sign; meals taken at the same table,
but so disposed as not to see the faces of those opposite to them;
religious instruction on Sundays received in a body; and a Sunday
School in the same manner, twice a day; both in Church and School the
same prohibition of intercourse; a full diet of meat, bread and
vegetables; comfortable bedding, in very narrow, but well aired, well
warmed cells, and the utmost attention to cleanliness in every
department of the prison. Visitors are admitted, but without permission
to speak to the convicts, who on their discharge receive a sum not
exceeding three dollars, without any relation to their earnings. Their
work is uninterrupted during the day, except by their meals, and is
generally contracted for by mechanics, who find the materials. This
enumeration is not one of what is merely required, but of what is
actually done. And the strictness with which these rules have been
enforced is such, that it is asserted, that among thirty or forty

working together for years in the same shop, no two of them know each other's names. Nothing (it is well said) can be more imposing than the view of a prison conducted on these principles."

In a report made by certain Commissioners to the Legislature of New-York, in the year 1825, it is said -- "The Auburn Prison, with the discipline enforced in it, presents the following advantages: -- that the sentence of the law can be enforced with absolute certainty, since the escapes must be nearly impossible, and conspiracy quite so: and an attempt at insurrection therefore hopeless: -- consequently, that the prison is governed with great comparative safety to the lives both of the keepers and prisoners, which, in case of insurrection, are necessarily in danger. The separate cells by night, and the silence preserved always, entirely prevent all contamination among the prisoners: thus, at once is excluded the great question of the classification of convicts which has so much engaged the attention of benevolent men in Europe and America. By this system every prisoner forms a class by himself, and to all moral and social purposes he is insulated. The novice in crime may work for years by the side of the most expert felon, without making any progress in the mysteries of criminality. The prisoners are compelled to work diligently and profitably, and are deterred from spoiling their work. And we may add, as an important feature of this system, that if any human means can, as it were, enforce repentance and amendment, it is this. The entire separation from all criminal associates, the sobriety of feeling consequent upon temperance and labor, and most of all -- the sadness of solitude, most frequently make serious impressions. We have seen manifest proofs of such impressions among the prisoners, and only wish there were reason to expect they would be permanent."

In 1827, other Commissioners say -- "We consider that the Auburn Prison, with its government and discipline, is much better calculated to effect the intended purposes than any other which we have heard, or have any knowledge of."

The Directors of the Maryland Penitentiary, in reporting to the

Legislature of that State in the year 1828, advert to the "excellent discipline of the prisons at Auburn and Sing Sing." They remark, that "the experience of those prisons has afforded numerous instances of reformation to prove that their discipline combines all the advantages ever expected from the system, and is perhaps as perfect as prison discipline can or need be. Their principal regulations are few and simple, tending all to the maintenance of silence among the convicts, and, indirectly through this medium, to the preservation of order, security and subordination. Their discipline now serves as a model to all new prisons, and is well worthy the imitation of those of the old, that can possibly be adapted to its reception..."

Having thus exhibited the nature of the Auburn system of prison discipline, as well as of the Philadelphia system, the Commissioners have next to state briefly their reasons for preferring the former....

Both systems have warm advocates, and, as the extracts that have been made show, they are both in successful and satisfactory operation.

In making a selection under these circumstances, the Commissioners have been guided by sundry considerations, the chief of which are the following --

In the first place they were sensible that the people of Upper Canada, or at least such of them as had directed their attention to the subject, entertained a favorable opinion of the Penitentiary system which was in action under their immediate view; viz., the Auburn system.

Secondly, at Auburn, Sing-Sing, etc., we have, as the Boston Society remarks "a beautiful example of what may be done by proper discipline, in a Prison well constructed." Here it is said of officers as well as men, that "there is a place for every man, and that every man is in his place -- "We regard it," they add, "as a model worthy of the world's imitation." Captain Basil Hall too, in his book of travels in the United States, observes that he minutely examined this system and thought it deserved no slight praise. These are important testimonials in its favor.

Thirdly, The Auburn system is held in high estimation, not only
in the State of New-York where it originated and has been for some
time enforced, but has been successfully adopted in several other
States of the American Confederacy, viz., Massachusetts, Connecticut,
Vermont, New Jersey, Illinois, &c. It has also attracted the favorable
notice of other countries, especially of Great Britain, as the articles
in a recent number of the London Quarterly Review and other publications
fully prove.

Fourthly, The Philadelphia system can only be regarded as in the
course of experiment. The new Penitentiary at that city, owing to the
recency of its construction, has not yet afforded the means of deter-
mining its value, either intrinsically or comparatively. It is indeed
warmly eulogized and supported by its friends, and may, possibly, in
the end, establish a character superior to all other Penitentiary
systems yet devised. Nevertheless it has not attained to any superiority
over all other systems, except at home, nor has it been adopted any
where except in its native state.

Taking all these matters into consideration, the Commissioners have
come to the conclusion that the Auburn system is that which it is the-
safer to act on in this Province. They accordingly in recommending its
adoption by the Legislature, submit the plan of a Building which they
think will answer, and according to which so much only may now be
completed as may be found necessary, admitting of future additions from
time to time without injuring the plan, or impairing the
security or discipline of the Prison.... [followed by a discussion of
plans for the building -- including the number of cells, the kind of
work to be performed by the inmates, the expenses anticipated -- and a
discussion of a number of related questions, including the changes in
the criminal law that the new punishment of imprisonment in the penitentiary would require, the scale of punishments that should be adopted,
whether good conduct by prisoners should shorten their sentences.]

Signed: John Macaulay

H.C. Thomson

12 November, 1832

[This Report was accompanied by a number of documents, including correspondence between the Commissioners and William Powers, Deputy Keeper of Auburn. The Commissioners requested information on numerous matters of detail from Powers: the following is part of his reply.]

GENTLEMEN,

Agreeably to the request in your communication of 31st July, I send you herewith a plan of a Prison calculated to accommodate with cells and shops, when completed, eigh hundred convicts: and also attached to the same, a plan of a Prison for females.

In submitting this plan to your consideration, it is proper, as you request, that I should explain, as particularly as may be, my views as to the advantages expected to be derived from the variations I have made from the plan of the Prisons at Auburn, Wethersfield, Sing-Sing, &c.

It is a maxim of sound policy, that a system, once adopted, and found by experience to promote, as far as is supposed to be practicable, the object proposed to be attained, should not be abandoned for doubtful theories.

This may perhaps be considered a good reason for not deviating, in any essential respect in the building arrangements, from Institutions that have been attended with such signal success as those above named. In answer to this possible objection, I would remark, that so far from abandoning the system, or any part of the system adopted in these institutions, the variations that I propose to make in the building arrangements are such and such only as appear from experience to be necessary, in order to bring that system into complete and perfect operation.

You are aware that the particularly excellent and distinguishing characteristic of the Auburn system is non-intercourse among the convicts, while at the same time, they are employed by day, in active useful labor. This is the grand foundation on which rests the whole fabric of Prison discipline. The security of the convicts, the safety of the keepers, the profits of labor, the hope of reformation, all depend

upon this one feature of the system. Indeed it is this alone that
distinguishes our Institution from some of the older prisons, and
prevents it from becoming, like them, an active and most efficient
school of vice. It is very plain to be seen, and our experience has most
fully shown, that, to prevent communication among the convicts, it is
necessary that they should be under the most vigilant and strict surveillance of the officers; and therefore, any arrangements that can be
made to facilitate inspection, must be considered as improvements of
no small importance. The healthfulness of the prison is also important,
and indeed a paramount consideration. These two all important objects
will, I think, be clearly seen upon examination and explanation, to be
essentially promoted by the variations, in the building arrangements
above alluded to....

[of his new plan] ...the greatest advantages will be found in the
facility of inspection, and the free ventilation and consequent healthfulness of the cells. First, of inspection, the distance between the
extreme cells, in a block of 800, five stories high, like that in our
north wing, (including a passway or slip through the centre, which would
be necessary in a block of such length, that access might be had from
one side to the other without going round the end) would be about 370
feet. A keeper standing in the centre on one side, would be 185 feet
from either extremity, and would besides have the disadvantage of
being only on one side; while on the new plan, a keeper standing in
the centre, would be only 86 feet from the extreme cells, and elevated
upon a floor as high as the middle or third story, would be able to
see every gallery and every cell door in the whole block, and hear any
noise that might be made, even the lowest tone, in an attempt to
converse or communicate from one cell to another. It is therefore
demonstrably clear, that the facilities for inspection or surveillance
of the convicts (without taking into consideration the advantages of
the avenue between the ranges of cells which I shall presently explain)
are more than four times greater on the new plan than on the old. When
the convicts are marching to and from their cells, upon long galleries
like those in our north wing and in the Sing-sing Prison, the opportunity
for communication is unavoidable, as there is no position that a keeper
can take from which he can see them any considerable distance, as they
pass along the galleries. Their opportunity for intercourse is much

greater here than in any other place in the prison. On the new plan
this evil would be entirely obviated, as a keeper, occupying the central
position just described, could distinctly see each convict as he walked
along the gallery till he entered his cell. As it regards the avenue
between the ranges of cells, a brief explanation will show it to be
important. In the first place, it serves to separate the convicts on
opposite galleries from each others view. This is indispensably
necessary, to prevent intercourse -- it is true this might be effected
by a single partition; but by making the partition double, with a
space of two and a half feet between, with small apertures on each side
to look through, an avenue would be made in which a keeper could pass
along and look into every cell, unseen by the convicts. It will be
observed, by looking at the drawing, that the space between the two
ranges of cells is 20 feet wide -- an avenue of three feet in width,
through the centre, would leave a space on each side between it and the
cells, of eight and a half feet -- now by raising the floor of the
avenue four feet higher than the floor of the lower tier of cells, a
keeper in the avenue could distinctly see, through the apertures
above mentioned into two galleries on each side; that is, by passing
along on one floor of the avenue, he could inspect four tiers of cells;
and then by stepping up to another floor of the avenue, he would have
the same convenience for inspecting four other tiers of cells, so
that they would need to be only three floors in the avenue to enable a
keeper, himself unseen, to look into every cell and watch the movements
of each convict.

Convicts will always embrace every opportunity for communication,
and when cut off from intercourse by conversation, they will as far as
possible resort to signs and writing, when at their labor they have
little or no opportunity for communication in any way, on account of
the watchfulness of the keepers in the shops and in the avenue; but
they have access to paper frequently (different kinds of wrapping
paper for instance) and pencils made use of in the shops, which they
sometimes manage to take secretly to their cells, and attempt
communication by handing a writing to each other, or leaving it where
it can be picked up as they pass along the galleries, or in any other
way in which they think that they shall escape detection, such offences
for which they have no opportunity in the shops, are committed or

attempted in the cell -- while the convict is thus engaged, in writing
for instance, the keeper as he passes the cell door is generally discovered by the convict before the convict is seen by him. Although the
convict cannot see the keeper, till he comes in front of his cell,
still the keeper is seen in his approach by other convicts, who by a
cough or some other signal which they understand, can give notice that
a keeper is near. In this way they are enabled frequently, and perhaps
generally, to escape detection: sometimes also, mischievous convicts
are disposed to make themselves sport, and break the rules of the Prison
by attempting to talk to each other, or harrass and perplex the keeper
by making noises in their cells, such as speaking out a few words
audibly, or singing, whistling, &c.; and although the keeper may know
within a few cells whence the noice proceeds, yet the convict will
frequently pass unpunished a long time, because the keeper cannot
ascertain precisely and certainly which cell the disorder proceeds
from, by approaching it undiscovered.

It is easy to perceive that these evils and disorders of every
sort might be effectually prevented, by means of the avenue
above described, as the convicts in every cell could be watched by the
keeper, and the keeper not be seen at all by any convict....

42. Report of the Inspectors of the Provincial Penitentiary, 1835

   Journal of the House of Assembly (1835), Appendix no. 19, pp. 1-8

The Inspectors appointed under the authority of an Act passed on
the 6th day of March, 1834, entitled, "An Act to provide for the
"maintenance and government of the Provincial Penitentiary erected
near "Kingston, in the Midland District," in pursuance of the said
Act, have the honour

MOST RESPECTFULLY TO REPORT,

That they met at Kingston on the second day of August, 1834,
and after reading the instrument dated the 28th day of the previous
month, by which they had been appointed, they proceeded to organize
their Board, by the selection of John Macaulay, Esquire, as its
President, and of Mr. Francis Bickerton, recently in the employment
of the Commissioners, as its Clerk.

Finding that no funds had been assigned by the Legislature, in
the Session of 1834, for the maintenance of the Penitentiary, and
that none could be obtained for that purpose from the Executive
Government, the Board necessarily remained inactive until the month
of April last, when the sum of three thousand pounds was granted for
the "completion of the Kingston Penitentiary," the maintenance of
convicts, and the compensation of the Warden and other officers and
persons employed in the government and police of the Prison.

Thus supplied with means, the Board authorized the Warden to
make all the requisite preparations for the reception of such convicts
as His Majesty's Judges might, in the administration of the criminal
law during the ensuing summer, sentence to hard labour under the
discipline established in the Penitentiary.

Mr. William Powers, recently employed by the Commissioners in
superintending the construction of the Prison, was on the recommendation
of the Board, appointed Deputy Warden.

Three of the most competent candidates for the office of Keeper,
were engaged by the Warden, with the approbation of the Board; and

the names of six Watchmen were reported by the Inspectors, conformably to the eighth section of the Statute of 1834, which authorizes your Excellency "to procure a guard."

These Watchmen were placed under the orders of a Captain or Police Officer, who was also required to perform the duty of Keeper.

The compensation allowed the Keepers was fixed at eighty pounds, and that of the Watchmen at sixty pounds per annum.

The construction of the wooden fence, intended by the recent Statute, as a temporary substitute for a substantial boundary to be hereafter put up, was contracted for, and soon completed under the eye of the Warden.

Seven stands of arms were borrowed from His Majesty's ordnance stores, until suitable equipments for the Watchmen could be imported from England.

The quality and daily quantity of food to be allowed for the sustenance of convicts was considered and established nearly in conformity to the scale of allowances observed at the Auburn Prison, in the State of New York; and contracts were concluded for the supply of clothing, bedding, furniture, cooking utensils, and sundry other indispensable articles.

On the 27th day of May, the Warden reported to the Board the arrival of five convicts from the Home District, under sentence to confinement in the Penitentiary, whom it was found necessary to secure in the common gaol of the Midland District, guarded by two of the Watchmen, until the 1st day of June, when the Warden was enabled to take them into his own charge at the Prison, and set them at hard labour, under the rules and regulations adopted, and ordered by the Board to be strictly enforced.

Between the 1st day of June and the 30th day of September (when the fiscal year, so far as relates to the Prison, terminates,) fifty other convicts were received into his charge by the Warden, making in all fifty-five. Of these

```
The Home District sent                               6
The Gore        "      " (including 3 females).....  23
The Western     "      " .........................    5
The Niagara     "      " .........................    7
The Eastern     "      " .........................    1
The Newcastle   "      " .........................    1
The Johnstown   "      " .........................    1
The London      "      " .........................    3
The Midland     "      " .........................    8
                                                    ___

                              Total ........  55
```

Between the 1st and 31st day of October inclusive,

```
The District of Prince Edward sent ............   1
The Home District sent .......................    6
                                                 ___

                          Making Total ........  62 convicts
```

received at the Penitentiary within the present year, of whom three
are persons of colour.

The Warden's Return marked A. furnishes additional particulars
respecting the name, sentence, and term of confinement of each
convict in his custody on the first day of October.

The Return marked Aa. continues that statement from the 1st day
of October unto the date of the present Report.

Of the total number of convicts three are females, and the
remaining fifty-nine are males.

Their classification, as respects their nativity, stands thus: --

```
Natives of Ireland ..........................  16
   "     of Upper Canada ....................  15
   "     of England .........................  11
   "     of United States ...................  10
   "     of Lower Canada ....................   5
   "     of Scotland ........................   2
   "     of Holland .........................   1
   "     of Poland ..........................   1
   "     of India ...........................   1
                                              ___
                                               62
```

The ages of the prisoners are as follows: --

```
From 15 to 20 years, ....................... 16
  "  21 to 25   "   ......................... 9
  "  26 to 30   "   ......................... 16
  "  31 to 35   "   ......................... 8
  "  36 to 40   "   ......................... 3
  "  41 to 45   "   ......................... 4
  "  46 to 50   "   ......................... 3
  "  51 to 55   "   ......................... 2
  "  56 to 60   "   ......................... 1
                                            ──
                                            62
```

The abstract of the sentences is as follows: --

```
For 1 year  ................................. 9
  " 2 years ................................. 15
  " 3 years ................................. 17
  " 4 years ................................. 3
  " 5 years ................................. 15
  " 6 years ................................. 3
                                            ──
                                            62
```

In consequence of the manner in which the certificates of the sentences presented to the Warden with the convicts have been drawn up, the precise offence committed in each case cannot be distinctly set forth on the Records of the Penitentiary. The following is the only abstract that can be prepared in this particular.
Convictions for: --

```
Grand Larceny ............................. 37
Horse Stealing ............................ 9
Uttering Forged Notes ..................... 4
Arson ..................................... 2
Sheep Stealing ............................ 2
Petty Larceny ............................. 2
Felony .................................... 1
Returning from Banishment ................. 1
Forgery ................................... 1
Assault, with intent to murder ............ 1
Horse Stealing and receiving Stolen Goods .. 1
Grand and Petty Larceny ................... 1
                                          ──
                                          62
```

The regulation which is in force in the State of Kentucky on this head, may probably be found to merit the notice of our Legislature. It is this:

"In order that the nature of the offence, and the former character and conduct of the convicts may be known, the law directs, that the Court

before whom any conviction takes place, shall furnish the Keeper of the
Penitentiary with a brief statement of the circumstances connected with
the crime committed by each prisoner; such Reports are required to
be inserted in the Prison Register."

The undermentioned particulars relative to the convicts are
gathered from their own statements, which possibly are not in all
respects entitled to implicit reliance. They are, however, considered
interesting in other countries, and for that reason have been
collected here, under the direction of the Inspectors.

```
Under the influence of spirits when the crime
     was committed ...........................................  35
Intemperate Parents .........................................   2
Parents died before convict was ten years of age ...........   1
Parents died before convict was fifteen years of age .......   5
Instructed in a Sunday School ...............................  32
In the daily habit of reading the Bible ....................  13
Know the decalogue ..........................................  14
Observed the Sabbath ........................................  27
Single ......................................................  33
Married .....................................................  25
Widow .......................................................   1
Widowers ....................................................   3
Husband or wife died previous to conviction ................   4
Left husband or wife before conviction .....................   9
Lived with husband or wife when arrested ...................  16
Lived in adultery ...........................................   2
Had been educated at a College .............................   1
Had common education ........................................  21
Had inferior education .....................................  27
Are uneducated ..............................................  13
Can read ....................................................  21
Can read and write ..........................................  30
Were excessively intemperate ...............................   6
Were moderately intemperate ................................  12
Were intemperate ............................................  11
Were temperate drinkers ....................................  26
Were abstinent ..............................................   6
Had learned trades ..........................................  19
Had begun to learn trades ..................................   8
Followed trades when convicted .............................  13
Were owners of real estates ................................  16
                                                             ──
Professed to belong to the Church of England ...............  24
    "           "           "       of Scotland ............   2
    "           "           "       of Rome ................  15
    "      to be Presbyterians .............................   4
    "        "  Methodists .................................   6
    "        "  Baptists ....................................   1
    "      to belong to no Church ..........................  10   62
                                                             ──   ──
```

Had children who were under ten years of age 22
Had children who were above ten years of age 11

The report of the Warden, which is hereunto appended, explains in what manner, and to what objects, the labour of the prisoners has been applied; the amount, quality, and cost of each prisoner's daily rations; the description and cost of the clothing, with other details of his proceedings and management.

The statement marked B. is an estimate framed by the Warden, of the value of the labour performed by the convicts, under various heads, as therein specified, amounting to Ł234 13s.

This labour may be considered as directly productive to the Province, since it has been principally applied to the fitting up of the Prison, and is thus equivalent to an express appropriation of the same sum of money towards that object from the public funds.

The statement marked C. exhibits the several descriptions of labour on which the convicts were engaged on the first day of October.

By the accounts of the Warden for the year, ending on the 30th September, -- a copy of which has been transmitted to your Excellency by that Officer, in due conformity to the statute, -- it will be seen that the sum disbursed was Ł1830 15 6 1/2 including the payment of various accounts for services performed under the late Commissioners, whose duties have been transferred to this Board; and that the sum remaining unexpended on the first day of October, including the balance received from the Commissioners, money found upon the persons of convicts, rents, &c. was Ł1,220 3 9. This amount will scarcely suffice to defray the current expenses of the Prison until the month of February next.

The number of convicts sentenced during the present year is twice as great as was anticipated by the Board, and the current disbursements of the Warden are of course correspondingly augmented beyond the estimate.

In consequence of this sudden concentration within the boundaries
of the Prison of so large a number of criminals, many of them daring
and desperate, and all unsubdued in temper, and strangers to the restraints of discipline, the Board felt the importance of impressing on
their minds the hopelessness of attempting to escape, by adopting every
means at their disposal for preventing all conspiracies for mutual
aid and co-operation in their insurrectionary schemes. This point was
the more urgent, since the yard was surrounded merely by a plank fence,
and the prisoners might think it practicable to break through it, if
they did not see that they were at all times watched by a sufficient
force.

The Warden was accordingly authorized to engage two more Keepers
and six more Watchmen....

The Physician has been in regular attendance since his services
were required, and his salary has been recommended, for commencement on
first October instant, at the rate of one hundred pounds per annum.

The appointment of a Chaplain has not yet been made; Prayers are
in the mean time read by the Warden, as stated in his report, at
the close of each day when the convicts are in their cells. The want
of a Chaplain is nevertheless sensibly felt; his labours are most
important to the due effect on the convicts heart of the system of
discipline enforced in the prison, and would necessarily be unremitting.
To this duty not every individual in holy orders is competent.

The Inspectors feel most anxious that the Chaplain appointed to the
Penitentiary should not only possess a full share of learning and
talents, but also the zeal and devotion to the cause he is engaged in,
without which little that is really beneficial can be looked for at
his hands.

It appears by the lucid and comprehensive Report of William
Crawford, Esquire, the British Commissioner recently employed to
examine the American Gaols, that far greater efforts are made in
England than in the United States of America to impress on the minds
of the unhappy and depraved inmates of prisons, a suitable sense of

religion and virtue. Mr. Crawford's observations on this matter
appear to the Board so just and forcible, that no apology can be required
for submitting them to the particular notice of the Provincial Parliament. In adverting to the religious instructions of persons confined
in prisons, he says: --

"As personal reformation, to be permanent, must be founded on
Christian principles, so no system of prison discipline can be effectual
in which religious instruction does not form a prominent part.

The Prisons of this country, (England,) have great advantages
over those of the United States, in the means afforded by the Legislature, for imparting religious instruction; but notwithstanding the
liberal remuneration authorized by law, there are too many instances
in which Chaplains, having other professional engagements, do not
devote themselves exclusively to the duties of the Prison. On the
importance of this subject it is impossible too earnestly to dwell.

The vice and depravity to be found in every gaol has led to an
impression, by far too general, that most criminals are beyond the
reach of reformation. Whatever may be the fact, I feel assured that
the trial has in few prisons been fairly made. There can be no limits
to the sacred influence of religious impressions upon the hearts of
even the most guilty, and I cannot doubt that by the employment of
measures adequate to the occasion, minds, however hardened, may be
raised from degradation and reclaimed by the power of the Gospel.

When the number of the prisoners is considered, the whole time
and undivided attention of a Chaplain should be devoted to his dutues.

Whatever necessity prevails in the world at large for moral and
religious education, is immeasurably increased in a Prison by the
character and habits of its inmates, and by the disadvantages under
which that instruction can ordinarily be conveyed.

The situation of a young criminal, on his first entrance into a
gaol, might be rendered eminently favourable to good impressions; nor
can any human being, however hardened, be so debased by guilt as to
justify the withdrawal of the means which are necessary to his moral
restoration. Valuable, however, as are the public services of religion,
their effects on prisoners are in general but partial and unsatisfactory.

The labours of the Chaplain should not, therefore, be confined
to the performance of social worship; to this must be added private
and individual instruction in the retirement of the cell.

In his efforts to convince the misguided and reclaim the impenitent, sound judgment and knowledge of character are not less essential than ardent piety and persevering benevolence.

Against the numerous arts which prevail in prisons the Chaplain must habitually guard. A convict should not be allowed to hope for any temporal advantage, during confinement, from religious professions; nor ought a Chaplain to be exposed to deception, by having it in his power to procure for a prisoner any species of indulgence or reward."

The Inspectors duly appreciate the services which a Chaplain might render the convicts individually, and accordingly have it in view to assign that officer, when appointed, as many opportunities of private communication with each convict, as the general arrangements of discipline will admit of. Convicts should on no account be left without instruction or admonition.

In many of the American Penitentiaries ample room presents itself for improvement in this part of their system.

It appears that even at Auburn, where a Chaplain has charge who is surpassed by no other in worth or zeal, he cannot, under the existing arrangements, obtain a private interview with every prisoner under a period of three months.

The Board trust they will be enabled to introduce into the Provincial Penitentiary, regulations for the religious instruction of the convicts superior to those of Auburn, and even to emulate the good examples presented in England.

To effect this object it may become advisable that the Chaplains should not only be authorised, as at the Massachusetts State Prison, to take an individual aside at his discretion, and confer with him in private at any time during the usual hours for labour, as well as at the door of his cell, but also that he should be allowed a salary liberal enough for the support of himself and his family, and for ensuring the undivided application of his mental energies to the moral improvement of the criminals committed to his spiritual care.

The Board of Inspectors are engaged in framing a code of Regulations for the guidance of the Warden and other officers, a copy of which shall be submitted for the information of the Legislature.

This code is founded on the regulations which are now in force in some of the American Penitentiaries, and will be subject to such modifications as experience may show to be requisite and proper....

It is to be observed that the sentencing of females to the Penitentiary causes some inconvenience. They must be kept closely confined in the small temporary apartment formed over the present mess table of the male convicts, and occupying part of the area on a level with the fourth range of cells; and though their labour as seamstresses can always be turned to good account, they cannot be effectually subjected to the peculiar discipline of the prison until the separate place of confinement suggested for them by the plans and reports of the recent Commissioners shall have been prepared for their reception.

JOHN MACAULAY
President.

Penitentiary, near Kingston,)
   2nd November, 1835.   )

43. Extracts from the Report of the Commissioners on the subject of
     Prisons, Penitentiaries, etc. (1836) [The 'Duncombe Report']

     Journal of the House of Assembly (1936), Appendix no. 71, pp. 1-5

REPORT

of

COMMISSIONERS

on the subject of

PRISONS, PENITENTIARIES

To the Honorable the Commissioners appointed by order of the House
   of Assembly to obtain certain information, &c. Doctors Morrison
   and Bruce.

GENTLEMEN:

     I hope I shall not be thought trespassing upon your time or upon
the indulgence of the honorable the House of Assembly, unadvisedly,
when I again beg you to allow me to present some remarks upon State
prisons, penitentiaries, almshouses, houses of refuge, retreats and
prisons, the efficiency of which so much depends upon a correct know-
leges of the past, both in Europe and America, than some instruction
may be derived from previous experience and example for the benefit
of the future. I, therefore, visited these houses of punishment and
correction that were to be met with in the Eastern, Middle, Western
and some of the Southern States; examined the situations, and compared
their advantages with each other as places of mere punishment; as
places of reformation; of moral and intellectual improvement; enquired
into their financial concerns; how convicts were confined with the
most certainty and safety, and how employed most profitably, and at
the same time, with the least dissatisfaction to neighbouring mechanics
and laborers, and, as I anticipate to render more service to the
community in this Province by the information obtained with regard to
the great secret of the reformation of convicts, than in any other
respects I shall give you a brief statistical account of the penitentiaries, state prisons, &c. in the States I have before mentioned;
their prison discipline and its results upon the convicts, and upon the
community at large as authority for my opinions. I have given in the
Appendix extracts from the reports of many of the most useful penitentiaries in the United States, and the report of the superintendent

of the penitentiary in this province, at Kingston, to shew how much
the cause of humanity has been aided by the recent improvements in
criminal jurisprudence, and penitentiary systems throughout the civilized
world.

There are several systems prevalent in the penitentiary institutions
in the United States; -- that of Auburn, in the State of New York --
of Philadelphia, in the State of Pennsylvania; and the old penitentiary
systems still prevailing in many of the Western States. The whole of
the penitentiary prisons in the State of New York, and throughout the
New England States, are upon the Auburn system. Those of Pennsylvania
and New Jersey are upon the Philadelphia system, excepting the one at
Pittsburgh which is upon the Auburn plan. The essence of the penitentiary system is silence by day and solitary confinement by night.
The Auburn system combines seclusion, with work in company, under the
presence of coercion enjoining silence and the absence of all communication
among the convicts. The Philadelphia system combines entire seclusion
with work in the cell of the convict.

The most apparent results of these systems, or rather the
different practices of the same system has been: -- according to the
Auburn practice, a higher degree of profit from the labour of the
convict: -- according to the Philadelphia practice, a more subdued tone
of mind in the convict, and apparently a greater reform in his
disposition and habits; but less profit from his labour....

[Not all penitentiaries in the United States are run on these new
lines. Many in the Western states are badly managed].

The experience nevertheless, of some of the prisons of the United
States, whose discipline is the most exact and where classification is
an object of careful attention; and the growing experience of England,
and other countries of Europe, where the sanguinary codes which have
been for ages in operation, are beginning to yield in practice to the
more rational and humane substitution of hard labour -- restricted diet,
solitary confinement, and judicious classification, afford unquestionable
evidence, that the energies of the law in the suppression of crime, are
most potent and availing, when directed with a constant reference to

the moral faculties of our nature; and when clothed with that spirit
which seeks to restore, in order that it may safely forgive.

The great object of the institution of civil government, is to
advance the prosperity, and to increase the happiness of its subjects.
The agents of the government, become, in this point of view, the
fathers of the people; and it may surely be ranked among the duties
incident to this paternal care, not only that those who are guilty of
crime should receive the chastisement due to their offences; but that
no pains should be spared to remove the causes of offence, and to
diminish, as far as possible, the sources of temptation and corruption.
This obligation applies with peculair force to the case of juvenile
offenders; a class whose increasing numbers, and deplorable situation
loudly calls for more effective interposition, and the benevolent interference of the legislature.

Every person that frequents the streets of this city must be
forcibly struck with the ragged and uncleanly appearance, the vile
language, and the idle and miserable habits of numbers of children,
most of whom are of an age suitable for schools, or for some useful
employment. The parents of these children, are, in all probability, too
poor, or too degenerate to provide them with clothing fit for them to
be seen in at school; and know not where to place them in order that
they may find employment, or be better cared for. Accustomed, in many
instances, to witness at home nothing in the way of example, but
what is degrading; early taught to observe intemperance, and to hear
obscene and profane language without disgust; obliged to beg, and
even encouraged to acts of dishonesty to satisfy the wants induced by
the indolence of their parents -- what can be expected, but that such
children will in due time, become responsible to the laws for crimes,
which have thus, in a manner been forced upon them? -- Can it be
consistent with real justice that delinquents of this character should
be consigned to the infamy and severity of punishments, which must
inevitably tend to perfect the work of degradation, to sink them still
deeper in corruption, to deprive them of their remaining sensibility
to the shame of exposure, and establish them in all the hardihood of
daring and desperate villainy? Is it possible that a christian
community can lend its sanction to such a process, without any effort

to rescue and to save?

If the agents of our municipal government stand towards the community in the moral light of guardians of virtue; if they may be justly regarded as the political fathers of the unprotected, does not every feeling of justice urge upon them the principle, of considering these juvenile culprits as falling under their special guardianship, and claiming from them the right which every child may demand of its parent, of being well instructed in the nature of its duties, before it is punished for the breach of their observance? Ought not every one who has a just sense of the reciprocal obligations of parents and children to lend his aid to the administrators of the law, in rescuing those pitiable victims of neglect and wretchedness, from the melancholy fate which almost inevitably results from an apprentice- ship in our common prisons?

It is well worth the attention of the legislature to devise some means by which criminals may be speedily brought to trial after arrest; and while imprisoned for crimes in the common gaols of the different districts of the province that they should be classed so that the unfortunate debtor and the highly calpable criminal, should have no communication with each other -- Nor would I, if it were possible to do otherwise, allow criminals to have any communication among them- selves during their confinement previously to or after trial: and when sentence of condemnation to hard labor had been passed upon them, I would advise that the punishment should be carried into effect in the manner least likely to debase the human mind, and the most calculated to produce the reformation of the convict. I would still treat him as an accountable being, both to God and to society. His treatment should be just and consistent and as lenient as his situation would admit of. He should be taught to feel, that upon himself still, to a certain extent, depended his future prospects in life wherever the term of sentence admitted of a rational prospect of a return to society; and even where that was not the case, he should be brought to acknow- ledge that much of his present comfort or misery must as a matter of course, depend upon himself, -- and where he had no hope of enjoyment from society beyond the walls of the prison, he should be directed to

to look for happiness from within his own bosom here, and the hope of
future blessedness hereafter. He would then become a better man as a
convict -- enjoy more comfort in confinement, and be likelier, in
consequence, to be liberated.

The flogging in penitentiaries is highly reprehensible. Fear
should not be the only incentive to action -- convicts should feel a
respect for themselves; for the good opinion of the keepers; and
even of their fellows.

In the penitentiary at Frankfort in Kentucky, I witnessed a new
mode of punishment, that of suspended animation -- which appeared to me
to be better adapted to penitentiary punishment than any thing I had
before seen; for while it instantly subdued the most turbulent and
obstinate spirits, it neither debased the mind, nor left it in that sour,
unhappy and degraded state; the usual concomitant of corporal punishment.

This suspended animation was inflicted in the easiest and quietest
manner possible; without much loss of time, or danger to the health,
or injury of the convict, -- and from the short experience of this
institution upon man, and from comparisons long since made upon the
brute creation, it is admitted to be one of the most potent subduers
of the malevolent animal passions ever had recourse to. It is thus
produced: --

The convict is placed in an easy chair resembling the tranquilizing
chair, used in Lunatic asylums. -- The convict, sitting, apparently, at
perfect ease, has his feet legs, body, and arms, safely secured, a
box (or spout) with a box at one end of it is brought up behind his
chair. The spout stands upon three legs, and just high enough from the
floor to place the body of the convict on a horizontal line with it,
when his easy chair resting upon a broad bottom, shall be inclined
backwards so as to admit his head into one end of it. The sides and
partition next the top of his head are a little higher than the top of
his nose as he lies on his back with his head in the box. In that
position the collar is put down about his neck and secured. The
partition at the top of his head does not rest on the bottom of the
box by one inch; so that the water poured in will run out and be conducted

into a large pot or tub placed under the lower end of the spout to
receive the water. The keeper then takes a bucket of water and fills
the box until it covers the convict's face and mouth entirely, and
thereby suspends animation as long as may seem necessary to subdue his
passions, and on allowing him to breathe he has invariably become a
reformed man; with his turbulent passions quite subdued. He pursues
his work in the penitentiary without any of that morose and unhappy
feeling which so often succeeds the flogging, and other usual corporal
punishments that only restrains the convict by fear from the repetition
of the offence. Fear debases, never ennobles the mind, and therefore
should be had recourse to as seldom as possible, as a mode of punishment
in any system of improvement. In our civil or political institutions
teach children from their infancy to govern themselves: early
accustom them to the exercise of the moral and intellectual faculties,
thereby giving those organs of the mind an ascendency over the malevolent animal passions and propensities. Let all our literary civil
and political institutions be so conducted, that the organis of benevolence, veneration, conscientiousness and hope may predominate.
Thus shall we most effectually and permanently promote the peace,
prosperity, welfare and good government of this province.

All of which is respectfully submitted
CHARLES DUNCOMBE.
Acting Commissioner for obtaining certain information,
&c.   &c.   &c.

44. Extracts from the Report of the Penitentiary Inspectors and of the Warden with the 'Rules and Regulations' respecting the 'Discipline and Policy' of the Penitentiary (1836)

Journal of the House of Assembly (1836-7), Appendix no. 10, pp. 1-4, 19-27

...In their Report last year the Inspectors took occasion to express their anxiety for the appointment of a Chaplain, for they felt the truth of the observations made by the London Society for the improvement of Prison Discipline in their eighth Report.

"Although privation and restraint are indispensable as the ground work of corrective discipline, it must never be forgotten that the offender, although he may have forfeited his liberty, is still a moral agent, and an accountable being; that he has claims on the compassion of society which no misdeeds can annul; and that to raise him from moral degradation to present him the utmost facilities for cherishing repentance here and for promoting his happiness hereafter, are duties dictated by the best feelings of our nature, and enjoined by the sacred obligations of christianity."

The Warden and his Deputy do at present all within their power to awaken the moral feelings of the convicts, but their efforts in this particular cannot reasonable be expected to make any lasting impression.

A Chaplain only can duly attend to this part of the discipline; and the appointment of such an Officer has been already directed by the Legislature in the 7th section of the Act of 1834, passed for the maintenance and government of the Penitentiary.

The Convicts being allowed an hour at breakfast and another hour at dinner, which meals never occupy more than twenty-five minutes each, the remainder of the time is employed in reading the Scriptures or some religious tracts by such convicts as can read, and such as are altogether uneducated are then divided into classes, and taught to spell and read by qualified teachers, selected from amongst the other convicts, under the immediate eye of the Keepers and superintendence of the Warden or Deputy Warden.

This mode of disposing of the time of the convicts during their cessation from labor, which we believe to be peculiar to our system, is attended with material advantages; as while it allows to all the convicts necessary rest, it precludes entire idleness, and affords an opportunity for teaching the uneducated without interfering with the hours appropriated to labor, encroaching upon that time which, when a Chaplain shall be appointed, may be more advantageously devoted to their moral and religious instruction.

A considerable number of convicts, some of them advanced in years, and one or two of them foreigners, who, when they first entered the Penitentiary, were unacquainted with the alphabet, have in the short space of twelve months learned to read with tolerable ease portions of the Sacred Scriptures.

It will be seen that a certain sum has been realised in money as the fruits of a small portion of the convicts labor during the year just closed.

As soon as the North Wing and the wall of the yard shall have been erected, it will become important to determine to what objects the labor of the convicts shall be directed.

The Inspectors have not yet fully considered this point; but it is their opinion that the convict labour may be so applied as not in any degree to effect the gain of honest industry, or act injuriously on the interests of any class of the community.

There are many branches of mechanical labor which may be introduced into the Penitentiary with decided advantage to the public.

Should the mode of employing the convicts be hereafter taken up by the Legislature, and specifically regulated by statute, it would, of course, relieve the Inspectors from considerable responsibility and anxious deliberation.

The Inspectors, however, in making this remark, trust they will not be understood as desiring to shrink from the performance of any duties now required of them by the existing laws.

A copy of the rules for the government of the Prison, adopted by the Board, will accompany this Report.

JOHN MACAULAY
President.

Penitentiary, near Kingston,)
    October 22, 1836   )

WARDEN'S REPORT
To the Inspectors of the Provincial Penitentiary.

Gentlemen,

The number of convicts received into the Penitentiary since my last report is 43, of whom 41 are males and 2 females; a particular statement of which is furnished in the Return marked A.

The behaviour of the prisoners, owing to the strict enforcement of the discipline of the institution, has been such as to occasion little trouble in the management of them, the only offence worthy of notice, being an individual attempt to escape, which by the vigilance of the watchmen was rendered abortive.

It is to be regretted that the suggestions of the Board in the last Report, made to the Legislature, respecting the particulars of crimes committed by persons, sentenced to be imprisoned in the Penitentiary, have not been carried into effect, as much depends on a knowledge of the previous habits and character of convicts, in order to employ suitable means and treatment with a view to produce a reformation in them....

Reformation being the primary object to be kept in view in the management of convicts, and the knowledge of the Holy Scriptures being the principal means to attain that end, such prisoners as were altogether uneducated, have been taught to read, by convicts selected for that purpose, under careful inspection, to prevent improper communication between them: and, as an instance of the good effected in this branch of the operations of the Penitentiary, I would state that there are some convicts, who, on their first arrival here, could barely speak the English language, and another who could only speak in the French tongue, who are now able to read the Testament, in which they apparently take great delight.

The success of this undertaking will appear something more than common, when the almost unbroken silence of the Penitentiary, would seem to preclude the possibility of teaching the convicts a language which before they did not understand. It is worthy of remark, that the system of teaching uneducated convicts, as pursued in the Upper Canada Penitentiary, stands entirely alone. In all other Penitentiaries where the education of convicts forms part of the discipline, the only time devoted to that purpose is an hour each on the Sabbath morning and afternoon, and the teachers are taken from among the inhabitants of the neighboring towns and villages.

During the past year, I have continued to read evening prayers to the convicts while in their cells, and on the Sabbath days have read to them a sermon, with prayers and portions of the Scripture. Morning prayers, and a chapter in the Bible, are daily read in the prison after the breakfast hour by the Deputy Warden.

Whatever good may have resulted from these duties, still the want of a Chaplain to the establishment is seriously felt, as the labors of myself and the Deputy Warden, can only be directed in this respect, to the convicts collectively; whereas, to effect a permanent good, it is necessary that the moral and religious welfare of the inmates of this institution, should be studied and watched over individually, which can only be effectually done through the agency of a Chaplain.

As it was found impossible to employ the female convicts with any advantage to the institution under the direction of keepers, a matron was by order of the Board engaged in the month of October last,

under whose care their labors have been beneficially applied in making
and mending the bedding and clothing required for the prisoners....

H. SMITH,
Warden.

Provincial Penitentiary,
    October 15, 1836

Extracts from the RULES and REGULATIONS made by the Inspectors of the
Provincial Penitentiary respecting its Discipline and Policy, under
authority of the Statute 4 Wm. IV., ch. 37.

SECTION I.   Duties of the Warden.

...11th, The Warden shall take care that the Prisoners are treated with
mildness and humanity, and that no unnecessary severity is practised
by the inferior officers. If at any time the security of the prison
shall be endangered or personal violence offered by any convict or by
a combination of convicts to the Warden, or any of the subordinate
officers, or guards or to any other convict, -- or if any convict, or
several convicts combined, shall do, or attempt to do any injury to the
building, or any workshop, or to any appurtenances thereof, or shall
attempt to escape, or resist or disobey any lawful command, the
officers of the Penitentiary and guards, or any of them, shall, or
may, use all suitable means to defend themselves, to enforce the
observance of discipline, to secure the persons of the offenders, and to
prevent any escape.

12th, In executing the duties of his office, the Warden should never
lose sight of the reformation of the prisoners in his charge, and should
carefully guard against personal and passionate resentment on his own
part, as well as on that of his subordinate officers. All orders
should be given with mildness and dignity, and enforced with promptitude
and firmness. It shall be his duty to treat persons visiting the
prison with uniform civility and politeness, and, as far as possible, to
see that they are so treated by the inferior officers.

14th, No officer, or person connected with the prison, shall be
permitted to buy from or sell to any convict, any article or thing
whatsoever, or make with him any contract or engagement whatsoever, or
cause or allow any convict to work for him or for his benefit, or grant
any favor or indulgence to a convict, except such as the law may allow:
nor shall he receive from any convict, or from any one in behalf of such
convict, any emoluments, presents or reward whatever, or the promise
of any for services or supplies, or as a gratuity or emolument from
any prisoner committed to his custody, nor from any of their friends
or acquaintances, nor from any person whomsoever on account of any
convict.

Officers offending herein, shall be forthwith dismissed.

The Warden shall be vigilant in detecting infractions of this
rule, if any should be committed.

SECTION II.   Duties of the Deputy Warden.

1st, The Deputy Warden shall have the general superintendence, under
the direction of the Warden, of all but the pecuniary affairs of the
prison, and shall have the special direction of its police and discipline,
taking due precautions for the security of the prison, and the safe-
keeping of the convicts. He shall be responsible to the Warden for the
strict observance of all the rules and regulations of the Penitentiary.
    He shall be constantly moving about the different yards and places
of labor, without previous notice, to see that every subordinate officer
is vigilant and attentive to the performance of his duty, and that
the convicts are vigilant, orderly, and industrious.....

SECTION III.   Appointment and Duties of the Keepers.

...3rd, As the preservation and due effect of the whole system of
discipline depends upon the absolute prevention of intercourse among
the Convicts, the Keepers are to make sure of every means of preventing any such intercourse or communication.

4th, Keepers are prohibited from saying any thing in the presence of Convicts respecting the policy of the prison unless for the purpose of directing or instructing them in their duty. They are to hold no unnecessary conversation with convicts, nor to allow them to speak on any other subject but such as is absolutely necessary. They are not to take one Convict's word against another's, nor allow or countenance in the least degree one Convict, complaining unnecessarily against another; neither shall the word of one or more convicts be taken as sufficient evidence to warrant the infliction of punishment upon another; nor shall they suffer any Convict to speak lightly or disrespectfully of any officer of the prison. They shall require of Convicts, labor, silence, and strict obedience. They shall punish every convict, who is under their immediate direction and control, for all wilful violations of discipline and duty which they may discover. They shall inflict punishment with discretion, according to the nature and aggravation of the offence and in such manner and temper as may tend to convince the offender that his conduct has rendered punishment necessary, and that it is inflicted purely from a sense of duty, and not with the view of gratifying any vindictive feeling.

All violations of discipline or duty which Keepers may discover in Convicts, who are not under their immediate direction, shall be reported by them to the Deputy Warden with the name of the offender. At the close of each day, the Keepers shall report in writing to the Deputy Warden all cases in which they shall have inflicted punishment, with the name of the offender, the nature of the offence, and the amount of punishment inflicted: which reports shall be preserved by the Deputy Warden for the inspection of the Inspectors and Warden. Keepers, when on duty, shall govern themselves in strict conformity to the rules of the Prison. They must not indulge in whistling, singing, scuffling, noisy conversation or laughter, or in any act of insubordination or indecorum.

All Keepers, when within the precincts of the prison, are at all times to consider themselves on duty, and must govern themselves accordingly. -- When on duty in the prison, those Keepers who are in charge of galleries, shall remain in their respective stations, and not leave them for the purpose of assembling together and holding conversation. No arguments

or discussions having a tendency to excite passion or prejudice shall
be suffered in the Keeper's Hall. The deportment of the Keepers towards
convicts, shall in all situations be grave, manly, and discreet, in
order to inspire the convicts with respect towards them, and set an
example of propriety and decorum.

Their demeanor towards each other in the presence of convicts,
must be calm and respectful, without the least exhibition of petulance
or levity. They must avoid all conversation with each other or with
the convicts, but such as is absolutely necessary in the discharge of
their official duties. They must require from the convicts great
deference and respect, not suffering the least degree of familiarity
to be displayed by the convicts, nor displaying any themselves.

SECTION V.   Duties of the Physician and Surgeon.

... 8th, He shall report annually, to the Inspectors at the same time,
as is required of the Warden. He shall also, from time to time, examine
into the quality of the rations, and recommend for the consideration of
the Inspectors, such changes in the diet of the convicts as he may deem
necessary for the preservation of their health -- keeping always in
view that while the health of the convict is not to be sacrificed to
economy, the most rigid economy is to observed in so far as is consistent
with the health of the convict....

SECTION VI.   Duties of the Chaplain.

1st. The Chaplain, in all cases, and under all circumstances,
shall strictly conform to the rules and regulations of the prison.
2nd. He shall furnish convicts with no intelligence other than
what his profession requires.
3rd. He shall give them no hope or promise of aid in procuring
pardons.
4th. He shall be allowed free access to the convicts at all times,
for the purpose of imparting religious instruction and consolation.
5th. He shall endeavor to convince the prisoners of the justice
of their sentence, and explain to them the advantages of amendment,
and enjoin upon them strict obedience to the rules and regulations of
the Penitentiary.

6th. He shall freely exercise his own discretion in imparting spiritual advice, in such manner, and at such times, as he may deem most proper.

7th. He shall attend every Sunday morning, at 11 o'clock, for the performance of Divine Service.

8th. He shall report annually, at the same time with the Warden and Physician, for the information of the Inspectors: giving as consise and perspicuous an account of the progress and state of religion amongst the convicts as may be ascertained by facts upon actual obser-vation.

SECTION VIII. Duty of Convicts.

The statute directs "that all convicts in the Penitentiary, other than such as are confined in solitude for mis-conduct in the Peni-tentiary, shall be kept constantly employed at hard labor during the day time, except when incapable of laboring by reason of sickness or bodily infirmity and except on Sundays, Christmas-day, and Good Friday; and that it shall be the duty of the Warden to keep each prisoner singly in a cell at night, and also during the day time when unemployed."

Convicts are to yield perfect obedience and submission to their keepers. They are to labor diligently and preserve unbroken silence. They must not exchange a word with one another under any pretence whatever, nor communicate with one another, nor with any one else, by writing.

They must not exchange looks, wink, laugh, nod, or gesticulate to each other, nor shall they make use of any signs, except such as are necessary to explain their wants to the waiters. They must approach their Keepers in the most respectful manner, and be brief in their communications. They are not to speak to, or address, their Keepers on any subject but such as relates to their work, duty, or wants.

They are not on any occasion, nor under any pretence, to speak to any person who does not belong to the Prison, nor receive from such person any paper, letter, tobacco, or any other articles whatever; they are not to leave their places where they are set at work, without special permission or orders from a proper officer.

They are not to stop work nor suffer their attention to be drawn from it. They are not to gaze at visitors when passing through the prison, nor sing, dance, whistle, run, jump, nor do any thing which may have the slightest tendency to disturb the harmony or to contravene the rules and regulations of the prison.

No convict shall secrete, hide, or carry about his person any instrument, utensil, or thing whatever, without special permission or direction from a proper officer. The whole demeanour of the convicts must be correct, orderly, and in strict accordance with the established system of discipline.

They must not carelessly or wilfully injure their work, tools, wearing apparel, bedding, or any other thing belonging to or about the Prison, nor execute their work badly when they have the ability to do it well. For the wilful violation of any of these duties, corporal punishment will be instantly inflicted.

SECTION IX.   General Rules and Regulations of the Prison.

1st, from the 1st day of April until the 20th day of September, inclusive, the Prison shall be opened at a quarter past five in the morning and closed for the day at half past six in the evening. During the remainder of the year, the hours for continuing the Prison open, shall embrace all the day light.

II. -- Opening the Prison in the Morning.
Fifteen minutes before the time for opening the prison, the Keeper, or Watchman, on night duty in the Keepers' Hall, shall ring a bell, or sound a horn (as may be directed), as a signal to Keepers and Watchmen, to muster at the Keepers' Hall.

When the precise minute arrives, a small bell shall be rung, on which (the Keepers having taking their keys from the key room, and the Warden, or Deputy Warden, having ascertained from the keyroom and duty board, that the requisite number of the keepers and watchmen is present,) the watchmen shall repair to their posts, and each Keeper who has charge of a gallery or company of convicts, shall repair to his gallery and unlock the doors of the cells. The several keys shall be handed to the Keeper of the Hall, whose duty it shall be to replace them in the key-room.

The convicts shall come out of their cells in regular order, and march with their faces inclined towards the Inspection Avenue (each Gallery Company) successively, to the Docks, where they shall empty the contents of their night tubs, cleanse them well by rinsing them, than partly filling them with water, they shall march to the place where they shall deposite their tubs, in rows for the day; and each Company proceed in the same regular order to its respective shop or place of occupation, and commence the labor of the day.

About one hour after the opening of the prison, or at such time as shall be found most proper, a bell shall be rung by the direction of Keeper, in the kitchen, as a signal for the breakfast, on which the convicts shall break off from work, form again in line, and march under the eye of their respective Keepers, with their faces inclined towards the Avenues, to the Mess Room; each one as he arrives at his place, taking his seat with his face towards the table opposite his plate. When all shall have gotten their places, the Steward shall ring a small bell, and the convicts shall commence eating their meals, which shall have been equally apportioned by the Cooks; but as some may require more food than others, Convict Waiters, provided with proper vessels, shall pass along between the tables, taking food from those who raise the right hand, in token that they have it to spare, and giving additional supplies to those who raise their left hand, to signify they want more.

The Keepers shall give strict attention to the performance of this duty, by which the food shall be supplied in due quantities to all the convicts, without allowing them to impart to, or exchange with each other, which might create irregularity and confusion.

The Mess Tables shall be narrow, and the convicts shall be seated at one side only; so that never being placed face to face, they may have no opportunity of exchanging looks or signs.

When the Steward shall perceive that the convicts have finished
their meals, or have had sufficient time for it, he shall ring the bell,
when all the convicts shall instantly turn round, with their backs
towards the table, rise in their turn, and march in regular order to
the places assigned them for reading, or for instruction in spelling
and reading, during the recess from labor after breakfast; those to
march first who came in last, and afterwards the same order will be
observed in marching to their respective workshops and places of labor.

III. -- Closing the Prison at Night. -- Supper.

The bell for dinner shall always be rung at twelve o'clock,
and the mode of proceeding be the same as at breakfast.

Fifteen minutes previous to quitting labor, at a given signal
from the Keepers, all the fires in the shops shall be entirely exting-
uished; the convicts shall wash their faces and hands, and at the
ringing of the bell, they shall form in line in their proper places,
according to the numbers of their cells, and march in the order observed
on leaving their cells in the morning reversed to the place where their
night tubs are deposited, which they shall empty of the water left in
them, take in several quarts more of fresh water, to remain in their
tubs through the night, and proceeding to their cells, they shall take
their suppers with them, which have been previously prepared, and
placed in the Hall for them as they pass through it.

4th, When the convict enters his cell, he shall partly shut the
door, and as the Keeper approaches the door to lock it, shall suddenly
and promptly complete the shutting, in order to give the readiest proof
that each man is within his cell....

VI. -- Sunday Regulations.

On Sunday morning the officers and guard shall be all present,
and the prison shall be opened at the same time as on other days. After
emptying and rinsing their night tubs, the convicts shall be marched once
around the yard (if the weather be fair) for exercise, and shall then
be secured in their respective cells. A convict shall then be let out
by the Keeper from each gallery who shall take a bundle of clean shirts,

which have been provided for the occasion, and distribute the same among the inmates of the respective cells of the gallery, under the immediate inspection of the Keeper....

VIII. -- Divine Service.

At eleven o'clock precisely, the Officers and Guard shall be assembled, and the cells be unlocked, in the usual way, and the convicts marched through the place, where they shall be directed to deposite their water cans -- they shall proceed in the usual silence and order, unto the place prepared as a Chapel, and so seated as to confront the Minister, without looking into each other's faces. The Chaplain shall perform Divine Service, but there shall be no singing. The Keepers shall be so posted during the service, that they may be enabled to observe the demeanor of every convict.

The Guard shall be posted around the prison, during the Sunday devotions, as on other days.

The Keeper in charge of the kitchen, shall immediately after Divine Service, cause the Cooks and Waiters to prepare and divide the rations for the supply of the convicts until Monday morning. The rations shall be put into the ration kids, the water cans replenished with fresh water, and all shall be arranged in the usual manner.

When Divine Services shall have closed, the Company which came in last shall rise with their Keeper and march out, the other Keepers with their men following in regular succession, and as they again pass the place where their kids of rations, and cans of water are deposited, they shall take them up, and convey them to their cells, where they shall be locked up.

When all is secure, the Officers and Guard, except those on Sunday duty, may disperse and retire from the prison during the remainder of the day.

If any convict shall use, or accidentally spill the water in his can, and shall require more, a fresh supply shall be given him by the Keeper on duty, through the grating of the cell door with a tunnel....

XV. -- Furniture of the Cells.

The bedding, like the clothing of the convicts, shall be as the law directs, of coarse materials, manufactured (when it can be done) in the prison. -- Each cell shall be furnished with a stretcher or hammock, as wide as the cell, and six feet three inches in length, raised eighteen inches from the floor, and two blankets and two coarse cotton sheets of suitable size, and strong comb. During cold weather there shall be added a straw mattrass for each cell, with an extra blanket or rug. Sick convicts shall be allowed extra blankets, as occasion shall require. A bible shall also be furnished, according to law, to each convict confined in the Penitentiary who can read.

XVI. -- Shop Regulations.

There shall be at least one Keeper in each mechanical department, who shall be thoroughly versed in the branch of business pursued under his view; and in all cases, except when the Warden or a Contractor shall personally undertake the superintendence, it shall be the duty of the Keeper in charge to exercise a general superintendence over the convicts. He shall direct the management of all raw materials, and prevent their being wasted, and after critically inspecting all work, shall send it to the proper place of deposite with a bill thereof. He shall also keep an account of all articles, with the prices, and enter them in a book, which shall be afterwards posted by the clerk into the regular prison books under the eye of the Warden. He shall carefully instruct new convicts in their trade, and oblige the old to do their work well. He shall occasionally place a faithful and experienced con-vict by the side of an unexperienced one to teach him the trade, cautiously observing that they are so placed that he may easily keep them in view, and prevent any further communication between them than is strictly essential for instruction. He shall keep a list of all the convicts in his shop on his desk, place opposite the name of each the kind and amount of work done by him, and require of him all the work he can reasonably perform according to his ability, without assign-ing any stint-work or allowance at any time for what might be asserted to be extra or over work. No convict is allowed to ask, receive, or give, either by motion or otherwise, any information from or to another convice with regard to his work, without the express permission, and in the presence of the Keeper, from whom instruction when needed must be

demanded. Keepers on watch and observation in the inspection avenues
shall be vigilant to discover whether the convicts pursue their
various occupations with diligence, or have any communication with each
other, either by word or sign, and whenever any disorder is discovered, the same must be made known immediately to the Keeper in the
shop having them in charge. The convicts shall be so placed, and their
work benches arranged in the best manner to have their faces seen from
the inspection avenue and Keeper's desk, and as far as practicable
without facing each other. -- Convicts shall not be allowed to take a
position, or place themselves in such an attitude, as shall give the
Keeper reason to believe that they are holding communication, but shall
keep themselves so apart from each other as not to excite suspicion.
No convict shall leave the place assigned him to work at without orders
or permission from a Keeper. -- Seats shall be erected in each shop for
the Keepers, so elevated and conspicuous, as to command a perfect view
of the whole shop, and all that is done in it. A proper number of
convicts shall be selected for the shops as waiters, who shall distribute
and grind tools, sweep out the shops, remove rubbish, distribute
materials, convey manufactured articles to the places of deposite,
hand round water to drink, &c. under the eye and direction of the Keepers.

The waiters shall be so distributed that convicts may readily make
known their wants by appropriate signals. Water for drink shall be
brought by a convict, selected for this duty, from the Kitchen in pails,
which shall be deposited on benches near the doors of the shops, whence
drink shall be supplied as required to the convicts at work. Convicts
shall be shaved twice a week, in their respective shops, by convict
barbers, and their hair kept closely cropped. They shall also be
directed to wash their feet frequently, and occasionally bathe during
the warm weather.

The shops shall be often scrubbed and occasionally white-washed.
Raw convicts shall be employed on work for the public, until they are
so instructed as to be qualified for employment by contractors. In
other regulations respecting this subject, vide the Section relative to
the Duties of Convicts.

———————

VISITORS.

Free admission at the gate, between the hours of ten and twelve o'clock in the morning, and between one and three o'clock in the afternoon, each day, except Sunday, when visitors are not admitted, shall be granted to such persons only as are privileged by law to enter, and that all other persons (except under circumstances hereafter specified) shall be liable to the payment of admission fees, as follows: --

Male adults .... 1s. 3d. each.
Females and children .... 7 1/2 d. each.

Provided always, that individuals may be introduced free of charge, by any of the Inspectors, at any time, and that the Warden shall also be allowed that license. The Warden shall refuse admission to all disorderly or suspicious persons.

The Warden shall direct an Officer to accompany all visitors, on their inspection of the prison and yard, whose duty it shall be to prevent any infringement of discipline.

Visitors must attach themselves to the Officer attending them, and not separate into groupes, and straggle, or loiter about the premises. They must not be suffered to hold the least intercourse or communication with the convicts, by word, sign, or gesture, nor to converse among themselves, or with the Officers, in so loud a tone as to be overheard by the convicts. Visitors infringing the rules in these or in any other respects, must be immediately requested to return from the premises.

RECEPTION OF CONVICTS.

On the reception of a new convict, he shall be stripped of all his clothing, and his person thoroughly washed and cleansed, his hair cropped, beard shaven, and the prison dress put on him.

This service shall be performed by old convicts, under the immediate notice and direction of the Deputy Warden, or some Keeper. If the convict has any money, it shall be handed to the Clerk, who shall make a memorandum of the same.

The clothing worn to the prison by the convict, which is worth preserving, shall be properly washed, and kept for the convicts to wear on their discharge. If the clothing worn to the prison by a convict be valuable, and his sentence is for a short period of time, so that his clothing can be preserved without injury, during the term of his confinement, his clothing shall be labelled and kept, to be received again by the same convict, at the expiration of his imprisonment.

When a convict has been thoroughly cleansed, and dressed in the prison garb, he shall be taken to the Clerk's Office, and a description of his person, age, trade, or occupation, place of nativity, name &c. shall be recorded by the Clerk, in the Prison Register, after receiving such brief admonition as shall be given by the Warden, or Deputy Warden, he shall be put to such work as the Warden shall direct, who shall select that kind of labor, or trade, best adapted to his condition and capacity, and where his services shall be most required.

The Keeper, under whose charge he is placed, shall enter his name on his list. The Keeper having the charge of the cells, &c. shall see that his cell is properly furnished.

DISCHARGE OF CONVICTS.

By the 31st Section of the Statute, it is provided, "that whenever any convict shall be discharged, either by pardon or otherwise, it shall be the duty of the Warden to furnish such convict with necessary clothing, not exceeding three pounds in value, and such sum of money not exceeding one pound, as the said Warden may deem proper and necessary."

In accordance with the injunction of the law, such discharged convict shall be clad in a decent suit of clothes, selected from the clothing taken from new convicts, which is cleansed and carefully preserved by the Deputy Warden. He shall then be supplied with money, according to the distance of the District where he was tried and sentenced, but not exceeding the sum specified in the law. As the time when the convict is about to be discharged is favorable for eliciting truth, with a view to obtain facts which may be useful, the Chaplain will endeavour to obtain from him a short history of his life, his parentage, education, temptations, and the various steps by which he was led into a course of vice and crime, and commit the same to writing, for the information of the Inspectors: after which, the convict shall be discharged, with a suitable admonition and advice.

45. Extracts from the Annual Report of the Penitentiary Inspectors and of the Warden and Chaplain (1839)

Journal of the House of Assembly (1839-40), Appendix, pp. 57-65, 90-4

ANNUAL REPORT

of the

INSPECTORS OF THE PROVINCIAL PENITENTIARY, DECEMBER 1839.

————————

...The Inspectors feel that in expressing any opinion respecting the period of time to which the great majority of convicts are usually sentenced, that they are entering upon a province that belongs more properly to those whose very responsible and painful duty it is to award punishment and pronounce upon the criminal the sentence of the law; but if the end of all punishment be prevention of future crime, the question is open for the consideration of all who are concerned in the preservation of good morals, and in the reformation of the criminal.

Of late years the subject of Prison discipline has not only occupied the attention of those more immediately concerned in the administration of justice, but through the zeal and activity of Philanthropists aided by the praiseworthy and humane operations of certain benevolent societies both in Europe and America, much has been done to ameliorate the condition of the unfortunate prisoner. And something has also been done by means of moral and religious instruction during confinement, to reform the criminal.

The Inspectors however are of opinion that much greater progress has been made in that branch of prison discipline which imposes a

wholesome restraint on those vicious habits that led to the conviction
of the criminal than in the application of any means, for the preservation of the convict when discharged from the evil influence of bad
company and consequent exposure to those temptations under which he
first fell.

It is certainly much easier to restrain than to reform, and however
great may have been the improvements introduced, whether under the
separate or the silent system of prison discipline, the preservation
of convicts from falling into bad company, and to guard against a return
to those former evil habits, remains as yet, a desideratum.

The evil is seen and felt; but with all the salutary restraints
now in use, added to the moral and religious instructions placed within
the convict's reach during the period of his confinement, until a plan
is devised and put in operation to place him in a state of probation,
under some sort of surveillance after his discharge, little permanent
reformation will be effected and but little progress made in the
prevention of crime.

The Inspectors coincide with the Chaplain in his opinion of short
sentences, that they generally serve rather to harden and irritate,
than soften and subdue the criminal; and with regard to second convictions, whatever may have given rise to that "spirit of revenge,"
referred to in the Chaplain's Report, as inducing those unhappy persons
of whom he speaks, to return to their former evil courses, it affords a
melancholy proof how little they had profitted by the salutary restraints
to which they had been subjected, and the moral lessons inculcated
upon them during their imprisonment.

With regard to the suggestion hinted at in the Chaplain's Report of
appropriating "a moiety" of the convict's earnings to be paid to him
"after a stated period of probation." something of the kind has often
occurred to the Inspectors; but the difficulties which present themselves to their minds in carrying this plan into effect so as to
promote the true and substantial benefit of the convict, without prejudice to the public interest, appear so great, that it is with diffidence
they venture to bring the matter under Your Excellency's consideration.

On this subject however they would beg leave to observe, that
under the existing Penitentiary regulations and in conformity to the
present law, the convict, when discharged, only receives a few shillings
to aid him in returning to his friends; -- to whom, if they are honest
and respectable, and if he entertains any sense of the disgrace which
his misconduct has brought upon them as well as himself, he feels
reluctant to return in that destitute condition in which he is placed
when enlarged and sent out again into the world; and in this wavering
and undecided state of mind, while yet lingering in the vicinity of
the prison, he probably meets with some of his former inmates; it may
be some of those who had been associated with him in iniquity and
fellow prisoners in the same common jail before conviction. With them
he renews an acquaintance, and involved as they are in the same
common fate, they are led to look upon each other with a feeling of
mutual sympathy as the outcasts of society; to form a sort of community
among themselves, and instead of following up their original intention
of returning to their friends to earn a subsistence by honest industry,
they are but too apt to engage in some new criminal enterprize, by
which according to their system of morals, they may remunerate
themselves for their past loss of time and labor.

Under the evil influence of temptation from these associations all
their virtuous resolutions vanish -- they again put forth their hands to
steal; are detected, convicted and sentenced a second time, for another
series of years, to resume their former routine of labor in silence,
and to be placed once more under those restraints they had already
found so irksome and so opposite to their licentious and vagrant habits
of life.

While the Inspectors feel the necessity and importance of some
plan being adopted to place convicts on their discharge from prison
in a state of probation, they scarcely feel themselves authorised to
recommend any definite plan for effecting this object, however desirable.
With great deference they would submit, that if one-third of the
convicts earnings could be paid to him in annual instalments, on his producing to the treasurer of the District in which he resides, satisfactory certificates of good conduct, signed by any two magistrates of
that District, together with a certificate of some resident Minister of

Religion;   that he, (the convict) had been a regular attendant on his ministry during the year, and that to the best of his knowledge and belief, his character among his neighbours for honesty, sobriety and industry had been irreproachable, it might hold out such an inducement to the discharged convict to commence a new and honest course of life, and to persevere in his efforts of amendment as to be productive of the best effects. The Inspectors however, in offering this suggestion with all the objections that may be raised to its practical operation, and they are not without the apprehension that there may be many, again revert to their already expressed opinion of the inefficacy of short sentences to produce reformation.

The convict, during his imprisonment, is certainly placed under restraint, and is compelled to labor a certain number of hours every day, but he is confortably clothed, he receives a sufficient allowance of wholesome food, and though his lodging is small, it is well ventilated and every attention is paid to his health; so that he is not subjected to any bodily suffering or to any serious privation, so long as he does not violate the prison regulations; and under such circumstances the Inspectors are inclined to think that no sentence to the Penitentiary should be less than three years, and unless in cases where a sentence of death may have been commuted for imprisonment, the period should not exceed seven years; and in that event should it be thought advisable to appropriate a portion of the prisoners earnings to his own use after his discharge, under some such conditions as have been suggested, the years of his imprisonment should regulate the number of the instalments on which he should receive this appropriation, and the whole or any part thereof be made liable to forfeiture, in case of non-compliance with the conditions....

JAMES NICKALLS,

President of the Board of Inspectors
of the Provincial Penitentiary near
Kingston.

Penitentiary, Kingston,
   Dec. 1839.

THE WARDEN'S REPORT,

October, 1839.

To the Inspector's of the Provincial Penitentiary.

...Among the convicts now in confinement, there are 15 who have been received on their second and two on their third conviction.

The two convicts who are now confined for the third time in the Penitentiary, were in each of their convictions, sentenced only to 12 months imprisonment; a period too short either for the punishment of confined criminals, or to allow sufficient time to secure their reformation.

In some of the neighbouring states a law is in existence by which convicts after their conviction are, upon the commission of further crimes sentenced to the Penitentiary for life; and I beg to call the attention of the Board to this subject, in order, if it is judged proper, that it may be submitted to the consideration of the Legislature, whether the enactment of a similar law in this Province would not be attended with beneficial effects, not merely as punishment, but with a view of deterring discharged convicts from following their former vicious courses.

I am happy to be able to state that the general conduct of the prisoners has so far improved, that during the present year it has not been found necessary to punish to that extent which in previous years was required to enforce the discipline of the establishment.

The average number of convicts during the year 1838 was 153, while that of the present year is 151; and notwithstanding the near equality of numbers for the two years, the amount of punishment inflicted during the preceding year was at the rate of 50 per cent, above that of the year just ended, a certain indication that the discipline has improved, and that the officers of the institution have become more vigilant in their duty....

CHAPLAIN'S REPORT

To the Inspectors of the Provincial Penitentiary.

Gentlemen,

During the past year I have directed my attention to an investigation of the causes which led to the commission of crime, in order that I might suggest to the convict some considerations calculated to counteract the evil, and to operate as a safeguard against the repetition of it. I have found that Intemperance, is the prevailing cause to which crime, in a majority of instances may be referred. Out of 90 admitted since last report, 71 were certainly the victims of this ruinous propensity. The subjoined schedule will furnish a variety of particulars relating to the convict, as collected by personal inquiry.

The review of the past year affords some encouragement, for although the effects produced do not equal the labor bestowed, yet it is gratifying to learn that very favorable accounts have been received of discharged convicts, who regard their imprisonment as the happy means employed by an overruling Providence to rescue them from misery. It is with pleasure that I have to record, that several whose sentences expired within the last Eighteen months, have expressed their thankfulness to me for the change, which they believe was effected by their punishment. These cases of decided reformation however few they may be, still afford a reasonable ground not to be discouraged, though re-convictions frequently occur.

Two reasons may be assigned for the apparent inefficiency of the present system of prison discipline to prevent the recurrence of crime, especially when the convict has been but a short period before discharged. In the first place there is the shortness of the sentence: It cannot in reason be expected that a confinement of one year, can in the least weaken a habit which has "grown with the convict's growth and strengthened with his strength." The prospect of a speedy liberation naturally checks the rise of serious reflection, and engenders contentedness, indifference or apathy.

The case of a convict punished for the first act of guilt forms an exception. His mind is still susceptible of serious impressions; conscience still exercises her office; on such a subject a short sentence may produce the desired effect, but generally speaking the reverse is the case; and experience has proved it so. In the second place, a spirit of revenge actuates many of those who are recommitted; a desire to remunerate themselves for the labor performed while in prison, and for which they have received no recompense, impels many to attempt to enrich themselves by plundering others. Some have even so far acknowledged, that had they received anything at all resembling an equivalent, or had been assured that a moiety of their earnings would be paid them, after a stated period of probation; they would have had some inducement to continue in the path of honesty; but having once incurred the suspicions of the public, and feeling that some great encouragement was necessary to support them under so severe a trial; not possessing this, they yielded to the suggestions of an evil heart; unwilling to endure the struggles or rebukes of conscience, they then threw aside all restraint, and sought for consolation in the society of companions, who were like themselves indisposed to oppose a suspicious world.

To the question proposed to the convict on the eve of his liberation, "whether, in his opinion, the Penitentiary discipline is calculated to promote reformation?" this reply has been often given. "The fear of punishment, unless it be accompanied by the fear of God, will prove abortive." If this be not the preventing cause, every kind of punishment, whether solitary or social must fail of producing the desired effect.

To encourage this principle has been my earnest endeavour; public instruction on the Sabbath, and private admonition during the week, have been used; and it is a pleasing part of my duty to report, that the attention of the prisoners, (with but one exception,) has been readily granted.

The establishment of a Sabbath School, on a secure basis, would I am confident be made productive of great practical good; it is to be hoped therefore that the obstacles which rendered its operation impracticable this year just closed, will be speedily removed, so that a favourable account of its efficacy may be rendered in the next Report.

Through the liberality of the Tract Society, to which we are much indebted, a lending Library of practical Books, chiefly illustrative of the truths of the Christian religion, has been provided for the use of the Convicts: on their part, there is evinced already, an intense desire to obtain a perusal of them. Should nothing be gained but the diversion of their minds from scenes of wickedness which they would otherwise brood upon; for this result at least, we shall have reason to be thankful. One great thing to be desired, is, to banish evil thoughts, and this may be obtained by the circulation of Tracts and other pious works as subsidiaries to the Bible. The experiment is worth making.

I cannot conclude this Report without tendering my warmest thanks to the Warden and his Deputy for their hearty co-operation in all matters connected with my Department.

W.M. HERCHMER,

Chaplain.

October 1839.

[Chaplain's report on the inmates, 1839]

50 ..... Under the influence of Liquor when crime was committed

36 ..... Had intemperate Parents

27 ..... Instructed in a Sunday School

18 ..... Know the Decalogue

20 ..... Observes of the Sabbath

CONDITION

70 ..... Single

20 ..... Married

5 ..... Lived in Adultery

EDUCATION

2 ..... Academical

43 ..... Common

25 ..... Very poor

20 ..... Without

HABITS

21 ..... Excessively Intemperate
50 ..... Intemperate
9 ..... Temperate Drinkers
10 ..... Abstinent

EDUCATION

40 ..... Read and Write
30 ..... Read
10 ..... Owners of Real Estate

RELIGION

24 ..... Church of England
7 ..... " Scotland
23 ..... " Rome
3 ..... " Presbyterian
13 ..... " Methodist
4 ..... " Baptist
14 ..... " None

WHERE BORN

6 ..... England
22 ..... Ireland
5 ..... Scotland
22 ..... Upper Canada
4 ..... Lower Canada
24 ..... United States

46. From the Chaplain's Report, 21 October, 1841

Journal of the Legislative Assembly (1842), Appendix H.

Since the resumption of my duties on my return from Europe, I
have kept in view the primary object for which the Institution, with
whose Spiritual superintendence I have been entrusted, was especially
established -- the reformation of the offender; and to carry out this
important principle, I have based my efforts upon the unerring word of
truth: being well assured that no amendment can be permanent or
satisfactory, unless the evil by which the security of society has been
endangered, and the happiness of the criminal destroyed, be attacked
at the very root. Under this impression, the Convict has been directed
to regard his imprisonment, not only as a punishment for the injury
which he has inflicted on society, and for which he deservedly suffers,
but as a means designed to awaken reflection, and so to become instru-
mental, under God's blessing in the destruction of evil habits, and in
the restoration of the offender to that happiness which he has through
his own folly for a time forfeited. It is my persuasion that terror
never has worked reform; the fear of punishment may prevent a repetition
of crime, and may produce external respect to the established usages
of society, but the principle of the Penitentiary system reaches
further than this: -- it not only consults the safety of the community,
by enforcing its laws, but it provides for and aims at the permanent
improvement of the Convict. Its principle is 'love working by fear.'
My time, therefore, has been employed, and my counsel directed to the
practical operation of this principle; and I think I have good reason
to hope, that the majority of the Convicts regard their confinement
within the walls of the Prison rather as a visitation from Heaven,
designed to effect, through a temporary chastisement richly merited,
their future good, than as a retribution of man for offences committed
against his security and comfort. To all, the chastisement for the
present seemeth not joyous, but grievous; nevertheless afterwards,
I trust it will yield to many the peaceable fruit of righteousness.

47. From the Chaplain's Report, 1842

Journal of the Legislative Assembly (1843), Appendix G.G.

Many a Convict on his last interview with the Chaplain, previously
to regaining his liberty, has expressed his thanks for the privileges
of the Penitentiary [especially for instruction in reading]....

It must be admitted that our fairest prospects are sometimes
blasted in the re-commitment of once hopeful Convicts. Whilst this
will ever be a subject of deep regret, it ought not to be one of
astonishment. The difficulties which meet a liberated Convict on his
return to Society are neither few nor trifling.... No one will employ
a man who has been in the Penitentiary; and I believe it to be in no
way improbable, that some have no alternative besides a re-commitment
or starvation. To remedy a defect of this magnitude should be the
grand effort of the benevolent.

It must be plain, however, to all, that without removing the
obstacles from the path of the reformed, to his perseverance in virtue,
the Penitentiary system, must, in a great degree, fail of its end.

...Two points, however, seem to urge my plea [for more school
hours]: First -- The degraded state of the mind of the Convicts on
entrance. Second -- The shortness of the opportunity for raising it
to respectability -- consisting of the period of their imprisonment
only.

48. From the Report of the Board of Inspectors

Journal of the Legislative Assembly (1844-5), Appendix M.

The Board most heartily concur with the Chaplain in his remarks
on the necessity of establishing some place of refuge for the liberated
convict; in many instances, he is driven to his old haunts of vice
from necessity, not knowing where to turn his steps; and the small

pittance allowed him by law being exhausted before he is enabled to
procure work to support himself, speedy recommittals often follow in
consequence.

49. From the Report of the Warden, 1845

Journal of the Legislative Assembly (1846), Appendix G.

The number of recommitments during the past year has been 36,
of whom 7 were tried by the Civil Power. When convicts are discharged
from the Penitentiary, who have neither friends in the country or home
to which they can repair, they find some difficulty in procuring shelter
or employment. The sum of money given to them on their liberation (proportionate to the distance of the District from which they came, and in
no case exceeding one pound) is too small to enable them to support
themselves until they can earn a subsistence, and, consequently, many
are driven to resort to their former vicious practices to procure the
means of existence.

50. Extracts from the Report of the Inspectors of the Penitentiary and
of the Chaplain, 1848
Journal of the Legislative Assembly (1848), Appendix S
No. 1 -- REPORT OF THE BOARD OF INSPECTORS

...The Rules and Regulations for the government of the Penitentiary,
which the Board had the honor to submit in the month of August last for
your Excellency's consideration, and which have been approved, have
been found to answer their expectations; and the Inspectors are happy
to inform your Excellency, that the punishments for serious offences
on the part of the convicts have materially decreased, most of those
which it is now necessary to inflict being of the mildest description.

Many groundless assertions having been made that cruelty was practised in the discipline of the Institution, the Board, with the intention of putting a stop to such unfounded statements, on the 6th Feb. last, with the view of carrying into effect the resolutions passed on the 18th January last, on the subject of punishments to refractory convictions, "resolved that each Inspector shall attend in rotation, during one week, at the Penitentiary, at the hour of one o'clock, P.M." Since which time the punishments inflicted upon convicts for infractions of the rules and regulations of the establishment have been regularly examined into and sanctioned by one of the Inspectors, agreeable to the resolution quoted; and in justice to the Warden the Board beg leave to observe, that they have in no instance had reason to differ with that Officer respecting the nature or amount of punishment ordered by him in pursuance of the directions of the Government.

The Board fully agree with the Warden respecting the difficulty of preserving due subordination on the part of juvenile convicts, and they would respectfully recommend that in future no boys under 15 years of age be sentenced to imprisonment in the Penitentiary....

The Board have to regret that they cannot concur in the Chaplain's Report, that Officer appearing to take an erroneous view of their proceedings in the exercise of their powers and duties. In pursuance of the Statute before mentioned, the Board directed the Chaplain to attend three hours per day for the purpose of imparting religious instruction to the convicts, which is barely sufficient for the performance of such important duties; but even this limited time is not at all times convenient for the Chaplain to devote to such purposes. The Board cannot but hope that it may, at no distant period, be found possible to place the office of the Chaplain upon such a footing with regard to his salary, that his whole attention should be devoted to the spiritual welfare of the convicts under his care, which is far from being the case at present, as it is within their knowledge that several of the prisoners, on leaving the Penitentiary after a confinement of three years, have stated that they have not been favoured with any interviews with the Chaplain during their imprisonment.

In support of their opinion on this subject, the Board beg leave

to quote that of the late Rev. Whitworth Russell, who devoted many
years to the study of prison discipline, and whose remarks respecting
the duty of a Chaplain are, therefore, entitled to great consideration.

That Reverend Gentleman, on giving his evidence before a Committee
of the House of Lords respecting the duty of a Chaplain, says --
"the whole of his time should be devoted to the performance of his
duties. The offices of religion, such as prayer, sermons, and exhortations,
are altogether ineffectual when unconnected with religious instruction.
It is by enlightening the mind that permanent good can be effected;
and the mind can only be enlightened by a systematic and unremitted
course of religious instruction, which requires a large portion of
time"....

All of which is most respectfully submitted.

> THOMAS A. CORBETT,
> President.
> GEORGE BAKER,
> JAMES HOPKIRK,
> HENRY GILDERSLEEVE.

Kingston,
    15th January, 1848.

No. 2. -- REPORT OF THE CHAPLAIN.
To the Board of Inspectors of the Provincial Penitentiary.
Sirs,

In presenting my Annual Report, I beg to follow the order
suggested in Rule 13th of those just received; not only because it
will enable me to present systematically what duty to my office enjoins
on me, but also, thus early to protest against a code, which, if obeyed,
destroys much of the Chaplain's usefulness; and, if disobeyed, makes
him amenable to the consequences of disobedience.

The number of convicts under my spiritual charge, are two hundred
and ninety-seven. As to their progress towards reformation it is
extremely difficult to speak, except with diffidence. It is hoped
that much is doing beneath the surface of even that seeming indifference

which marks the conduct of many, which, at some future period, will
mightily influence them for good.

The Chaplain's public ministrations are attended to with the
greatest apparent respect and interest; and several have thanked him,
on their leaving the Institution, for the benefit which they have
supposed themselves to have received from them.

Were the Chaplain enabled to carry out those ministrations to the
full extent, which his judgment and experience convince him to be
required by the interests of the convicts: were the place of meeting
adapted to the making suitable impressions on the minds of the assembled;
much more would, it is believed, be done with the same outlay of
reformatory means.

But were those means, in any good degree, commensurate with the
end in view, which at present they are not: did the Institution contain
that moral machinery which other British Penitentiaries possess, but
of which ours still continues so lamentably deficient, despite the
earnest solicitations both of my predecessor and myself: had we a
School-master and School-room, Chapel and Chaplain, with, to
use the language of the first Board of Inspectors, "a salary liberal
enough for the support of himself and family, for the insuring the
undivided application of his mental energies to the moral improvement
of the criminals committed to his spiritual care." Had we all these
appliances, together with a due portion of every day to carry them into
execution; then, and not till then, would the Institution, over which
you are called to preside, be what it is yet hoped it will be, but which
at present it is not, "A School of Reform."

The hindrances to the convict's reformation are so many, and so
great, as all but to overwhelm the counterbalancing influence of the
Chaplain's efforts.

Even were all that granted, which duty has compelled him again
and again to ask, because demanded by the well-being of the Provincial
Penitentiary -- if the influence beyond the chapel and school-room
continue to be, what it is now, in so great a degree destructive of all
good impressions, the difference of time spent under the Keeper and

the Chaplain is so disproportionate, that the good gained by the latter,
would be sadly counteracted, if not destroyed, by the ill received from
the former.

The Board will, I trust, bear with me whilst I respectfully though
honestly refer to the report of February last, and the rules received
this present October, which I am, I suppose, to consider as the result,
in some degree, of that report.

The Chaplain had hoped that a thorough investigation of his office
would have resulted from the reception of that document, that some of
the difficulties there complained of would have been removed: but,
besides the granting one day more to the School, and a sum of money
for the purchase of a Library, nothing has been done: and even the
former boon has lost much of its value by Mr. Costen's services having
been necessarily withdrawn on his promotion to his present office, and
no adequate successor having been appointed.

The Chaplain holds himself in readiness to give, either in writing
or orally, a full and complete exposition of those several topics
mentioned in the report alluded to.

The Rules which the Board has just forwarded for the Chaplain's
guidance, as they contain little beyond the contents of a former code,
have already received the attention of that officer.

Their object seems to be, to concentrate all moral and religious
as well as physical power in one officer, thus virtually abolishing all
others. This cannot be done except at the expense of morality and
religion, if a distinct moral and religious office be needed. If
such an office is not required, then the Chaplain is a needless appendage
to the Institution; and the salary, trifling as it is, should be saved
to the community by the abolition of the office. If, on the other
hand, such an office is demanded by the united suffrage of all, who
have given the subject that consideration which its importance demands,
then that officer must be quite independant of such constant and minute
interference as that contemplated by rules 2 and 5; an interference
which would strip the Chaplain of his usefulness, in a very great degree;

and so degrade him from that eminence on which the framers of the
constitution of the Provincial Penitentiary placed him; and in which
the Act of Parliament confirmed him, when making his appointment or
removal independant of all else but the highest authority which the law
of the land recognizes.

The Chaplain cannot suppose that the law contemplated the
inconsistency of making him as independant, in his appointment, as the
Board itself and the Warden; and yet so dependant, in the manner of
discharging that office, as the objectionable rules contemplate;
interfering with a conscientious and enlightened discharge of his
office, by a system of supervision unknown in any other like institution;
and to which no clergyman, who is sensible of what is due to him as an
Ordained Minister, and no Chaplain, who knows what his duties are, can
submit to, without an injury which neither the one nor the other ought
to receive; and which, if imposed, by the last resort, in case of
appeal, his duty both to his God and his country, would compel him to
resign.

The Chaplain is so convinced of the necessity, to the well-being
of the Institution, for the independance of his office, of all interference in the manner of its discharge, that he would in further proof
shew, that the placing him, as these rules would, in a state of
dependance, must so far degrade him in the eyes of the convicts as
that they would no longer confide in him as their friend, and the only
check to what is but too common, the petty tyranny of inferior officers.
If compelled to be guided by such rules, he is, at once, placed on a
level with the humblest officer, a condition equally opposed to the
letter and spirit of the Penitentiary system.

The objection to Rule 1 is offered, not because the interests of
the Institution do not require so much as three hours daily discharge of
the ministerial office among the convicts; but from the position of
the Chaplain. The salary given, as well as the Act of Parliament,
evidently contemplating a portion of his time only, whilst this rule
virtually claims all: since, after three hours devotion to his
duties daily, his mental and physical energies would be well nigh
disabled from further efficiency for duties requiring unbroken energies

for their proper discharge. The Penitentiary, through the Board, demanding the entire energies of the Chaplain, and not allowing him a salary adequate to his support.

The Chaplain begs to submit the following report of the School as furnished him by Mr. Costen, the Head Keeper: --
REPORT OF THE PROVINCIAL PENITENTIARY SCHOOL,

for the year ending 30th September, 1847.

	White	Coloured	Total
Average number in attendance...	78	18	96
Ages, from	10 to 50	16 to 52	
Spelling	52	9	61
Reading	26	9	35

At no time, during my official connection with the Penitentiary, has the state of the female convicts been so satisfactory; which is attributable, in a great degree, to the unwearied efficiency of the Matron, whose firm but kind government and constant instruction, have produced effects so desirable; and the Chaplain ventures to hope, that the longer discharge of her arduous office may produce far greater good during the coming year: and, further, takes this opportunity of recording his opinion -- that serious damage would be done to some of the best interests of the department, if anything should occur to mar so hopeful a state of improvement.

I remain,

Gentlemen,

Your obedient Servant,

R.V. ROGERS,

Chaplain.

E. THE BROWN COMMISSION, 1848-1849

51. <u>The Globe</u>, 4 November 1846

Kingston Penitentiary

Lash! - lash!! - lash!!!

It appears from statements which are not contradicted, that from
200 to 300 punishments are inflicted on the Prisoners of the Penitentiary
every month. Supposing these to average 20 lashes, it follows that 1300
lashes are given in a month, and 50,000 in a year, a far greater amount
we are sure than the whole British Army and Navy undergo. A hundred
and fifty lashes must be given in this den of brutality every day the
sun rises. Who can calculate the amount of pain and agony, that must
be imposed in this Pendemonium. Who can tell the amount of evil
passions, of revenge, and of malice, that must be engendered by such
treatment? A penitentiary is a place where the prisoner should reflect
on the past, and be placed under such a system of moral training as may
fit him for becoming a better member of society. Will the lash do that?
Did it ever do anything but harden the person whose body was torn by its
infliction? Why is the Press so silent about it? The Montreal <u>Times</u> and
<u>Courier</u> first brought the matter before the public. Why is any journal in
the Province silent?...

52. The Penitentiary

<u>Brockville Recorder</u>, 12 November, 1846 (from the <u>Kingston News</u>)

This institution is at the present moment occupying a large share
of public attention. For some eight or ten years it has enjoyed the
singular fortune of being allowed an unmolested existence, not even an
enquiry having been instituted as to the success of the system of
prison discipline which its establishment introduced into the Province.
People generally seemed desirous of knowing as little as possible of
the internal economy of the Penitentiary, whether practically or

theoretically, and it was left to the sole discretion and care of the Inspectors and the Warden. But the smallest circumstances frequently produce the greatest results. A little one induced a disregard of the very common and very prudent maxim "let well enough alone". For a very special purpose it was deemed desirable to have the Parliamentary Act under which the institution had thus smoothly proceeded, materially amended, and the sanction of the Legislature was obtained for the amendments proposed. Their effect was to deprive the Inspectors of some of the powers which they had previously enjoyed and exercised, and to transfer them to the Warden. The Inspectors, we believe, protested, but it was of no use -- and there was no alternative but to resign; at least that was the conclusion at which they arrived, and they acted upon it. Following upon this a letter appeared in the Montreal Times, directing the attention of the Government to an alleged mismanagement of the prison; this was succeeded by others, and the public quietude with respect to the Penitentiary has been, through their instrumentality, interrupted to an extent proportionate to the indifference with which the institution had hitherto been regarded....

The letters in question, however, it is surmised, proceeded from no unpracticed hand. If the quotation in the last is a transcript of a portion of the communication addressed by the late Inspectors to the Government, setting forth the reasons for their resignations, justice to them requires that the past and present policy persued in the management of the Penitentiary should be enquired into by a competent commission. With regard to some of the charges made against the past management -- charges referring to matters of detail -- justice to the Warden requires that they should also be investigated although, even presuming them to be true -- presuming that an amount of corporeal punishment has been inflicted upon the prisoners equal to that which is asserted to have taken place, we are clearly of opinion that the question involved is not one necessarily affecting the character of the gentle-man at the head of the institution, but that it is one which is embraced in that of the maintenance of prison discipline. The Warden may, for instance, in view of the whole circumstances of the case of each refractory prisoner, deem a certain amount of corporeal punishment necessary; another may resort to an opposite method -- both having in view a like object, the maintenance of a due subordination among the convicts under their charge. But we are assured that even this suppositious or presumed case does not apply to Mr. Smith; on the contrary, that if he has erred, it has been on the side of leniency.

We can hardly doubt that an inquiry will now be instituted by the Government; let us add the hope that such inquiry will not be confined to the mere routines of discipline in the Penitentiary, but that it will embrace a matter of still greater importance -- that the question whether or not the establishment of that institution has tended to the reformation of criminals and the diminution of crime in the Province, will be included: Such an inquiry is of vast importance. It is one which has engaged a great deal of attention in the neighboring States, in the mother country, and on the continent of Europe, and is worthy of being pursued here. 'How to punish crime, and in so doing reform the criminal; how to uphold the man as a terror to evil doers, and yet at the same time be implanting in him the seeds of a future more happy and prosperous life, is perhaps the most difficult problem of legis- lation:' but the difficulty should stimulate to a vigilant surveillance of the operation of those means which have been adopted to work out a solution.

53. The Globe, 28 August 1847

The most barbarous acts have been charged against the managers of the Kingston Penitentiary. They are either true or false.... They [the public] have a right to know that every institution supported by their industry is conducted in a suitable manner, and that every modern improvement is introduced into its management.... The idea of reforming the unfortunate inmates of the Kingston Penitentiary, as far as yet appears, seems not to have entered into the management of that Institution. Until the principle forms a part, and a leading part, of Prison discipline, many acts of a vindictive and tyrannical nature will ever occur. Restraint and coercion seem the only means employed to maintain authority. The men in charge will generally be selected, from the highest to the lowest, from their fitness for the more harsh and

unrelenting discharge of what may be regarded as duty. Accustomed to
see their fellow creatures tied up and lashed every hour of the day,
as so many brutes, they become hardened themselves, although they may
have been humane when they entered the walls.

54. Kingston Penitentiary

   The Globe, 15 March 1848

   This institution, maintained at the public expense for the double
purpose of being a place for confinement and reform of criminals, has
been repeatedly before the public, under the charge of being a den of
cruelty, where the most savage treatment is given to the unfortunate
inmates, who must emerge from durance not subdued but infuriated, without
one ray of light infused into their minds to guide their future path
but confirmed and strengthened in their bad habits by the treatment
they experience at the hand of authority. New exposures have been made
by the Chronicle and News, of the workings of this sink of revenge and
barbarity: a letter is given from two convicts whose time is expired,
while such testimony should be received with due caution, the document
we allude to bears strong internal marks of truth. All that has been
published on this distressing subject shows that the whole system of
the prison is bad, -- that it is under the charge of those who are
utterly unfit for their situations, and that there is an absolute
necessity for a change....

55. The Globe, 11 September 1849

   The report of the Commissioners on Kingston Penitentiary will soon
be published.... The Commissioners had not been long engaged before
they found that the Institution was rotten to the very core....

The amount of labour which the Commissioners had to go through can only be understood by persons conversant with the multifarious departments of a large Penitentiary. Perhaps no one subject of inquiry presents so many points of deep interest and import at once as that of Prison discipline....

...it will suffice to show that the enquiry was not instituted too soon, when we state...that the punishments were carried to an extent frightful to contemplate. In one year, over six thousand punishments of all descriptions were inflicted, and in another no fewer than two thousand one hundred inflictions of corporal punishment are recorded -- not 2100 lashes, but 2100 floggings, in which the number of lashes varied from nine to sixty, for such offences as laughing, talking, and staring.

56. Extracts from the First Report of the Commissioners Appointed to Investigate into the Conduct, Discipline and Management of the Provincial Penitentiary [The Brown Report]

   Journal of the Legislative Assembly (1849), Appendix B.B.B.B.B. [not paginated]

   (A) A Summary of the Charges preferred against the Warden

I. Permitting irregular practices in the Penitentiary, destructive of the discipline necessary in such an Institution.

   1. Favouritism towards particular Convicts
   2. Giving food to Convicts between meals
   3. Permitting Teamsters, and all other persons on Business, to go among the Convicts unaccompanied by a guard

II. Mismanagement or Negligence reducing the Penitentiary to a State of the utmost disorder.

   1. The Convicts talk freely to one another.
   2. The Convicts get tobacco constantly by stealth.
   3. The Convicts steal from the Tradesmen coming in with provisions.
   4. The Convicts obtain intoxicating liquors by stealth.

5. The reformation of Convicts is unknown.

6. Articles made by Convict labour and public stores are allowed to go out of the prison, without a permit from the Warden or Clerk, contrary to rule.

7. The officers of the Institution have no confidence in the Uprightness of the Warden, and are deterred from doing any duty which they conceive will be unacceptable to him.

8. For years the Warden and the Deputy Warden (for the time being) were on the worst possible terms -- not speaking to each other.

9. The present officers are divided into two parties -- those in favour of the Warden and his family, and those against him.

10. Sundry transactions showing the total disorder prevalent in the Institution.

III. Culpable conduct in reference to his son, Kitchen-Keeper, F.W. Smith (6 charges)

IV. Gross Neglect of his Duties as Warden

1. In not visiting the whole Establishment daily.

2. In not being present when the Convicts were at Meals.

3. In not being present when Corporal Punishment was inflicted upon the Convicts.

4. In not taking means earlier to free the Cells of the Convict Women from Bugs.

5. In entrusting the examination of Convicts about to be discharged, to another Officer -- to one incompetent for the duty.

6. In not putting the same questions to female convicts and soldiers, as to male civilians.

7. In not taking an active part in the work daily going on in the Establishment.

8. In not taking an active interest in the moral condition of the Convicts.

9. In not being present at Divine Service.

V. Culpable mismanagement of the business affairs of the Penitentiary (13 charges)

VI. Gross negligence and incapacity, in regard to the books and accounts of the Penitentiary (8 charges)

VII. Starving the Convicts in the Penitentiary (16 charges)

VIII. Pursuing a system of punishment in the management of the discipline -- cruel, indiscriminate, and ineffective

1. In neglecting for many years, to keep a proper Record of the Punishment inflicted.

2. In the character of the several modes of punishment.

3. In flogging the same convicts for days consecutively.

4. In flogging convicts whose backs were unhealed from previous punishment.

5. In the disproportion between the offences of Convicts, and the punishments awarded to them; and the variableness in the amount of punishment affixed at different times to the same offences.

6. In the very great extent of the Punishment inflicted on the inmates of the Penitentiary.

7. In flogging women.

8. In the case of Alexis Lafleur. [age 11, 1842]

9. In the case of Convict Henry Cooper.

10. In the case of Convict Peter Charboneau. [aged 10, 1845]

11. In the case of the Convict Antoine Beauché. [aged 8, 1845]

12. In the case of Convict John M'Grath.

13. In the case of Convict Louis Beauché.

14. In goading, by excessive punishment, convict James Brown into a state of insanity, or in aggravating the malady under which he laboured.

15. In goading John Donovan, by excessive punishment, into a state of insanity, or aggravating the malady under which he laboured.

16. In goading Convict Narcisse Beauché, by excessive punishment, into a state of insanity, or aggravating the malady under which he laboured.

17. In goading Convict Michael Sheehan, by excessive punishment, into a state of insanity, or aggravating the malady under which he laboured.

18. In goading Charlotte Reveille, a convict, by excessive punishment, into a state of insanity, or aggravating the malady under which she laboured.

IX. Gross Misconduct as Warden of the Penitentiary (8 charges)

X. Making false representations (10 charges)

XI. Peculation (20 charges)

(B) Charge VIII, part 2 -- character of punishments:

From June, 1835, to April, 1842, the punishments adopted, were flogging with the cat-o'nine-tails, and flogging with the raw-hide. These were the only punishments for offences of all grades.

From April, 1842, to October, 1846, the punishments were -- flogging with the cats -- flogging with the raw-hide -- irons -- solitary confinement -- and bread and water, instead of the regular rations.

From October, 1846, to February 1847, the cats and raw-hide were suspended by the Government.

From February 1847, up to now, the punishments have been -- the cats -- shutting up in a box -- irons -- solitary confinement in dark cells -- solitary confinement in the Convict's own cell -- and bread and water.

From 1835 to 1847, neither the Warden nor the Surgeon were present at the infliction of corporal punishment; but in October, 1847, the following rule was passed: --
'Extracts from the Rules and Regulations for the government of the Penitentiary, October, 1847: --
Punishment of Convicts
The Warden and Surgeon shall attend at every infliction of corporal punishment; and the Surgeon shall certify in writing, that he has examined the health of the Convict ordered for punishment, and that it is such as to enable him to bear the infliction without detriment thereto; and without such certificate, the punishment shall not take place.'

(C) Commissioners' conclusions from Charge VIII, part 6, extent of punishment:

We have thus given the evidence at great length; though we are of opinion that no amount of testimony could meet the case developed in the punishment tables. The simple facts, that the number of punishments rose from seven hundred and seventy in 1843, to two thousand one hundred and two in 1845, and from three thousand four hundred and forty-five in 1846, to six thousand and sixty-three in the year following; the same number of men being subject to discipline in the two latter years.

That in the year 1845 and 1846, the number of corporal punishments alone, averaged between four and five punishments in each year, for every man, woman, and child in the Prison; and that in the same years there was an average of seven corporal punishments inflicted daily -- shows beyond cavil, that the system pursued has been one of the most frightful oppression.

The rapidity with which the punishments increase, from year to year, is particularly noticeable, the increase in the number of Convicts bearing no proportion to it. It is very clear, that the moment excessive punishment commenced, the hardening effect it had on the culprits produced a growing necessity for punishment, and where it would have stopped, had the Government not interfered and restrained it, it is impossible to say.

As many as twenty, thirty, and even forty men, have been flogged in one morning, the majority of them for offences of the most trifling character; and the truth of the complaint resting solely on the word of a Guard or Keeper, subject at best to all the frailties of other men. The exasperation which such a system could only produce, must have bid defiance to all hope of reform. To see crowds of full grown men, day after day, and year after year, stripped and lashed in the presence of four or five hundred persons, because they whispered to their neighbour, or lifted their eyes to the face of a passerby, or laughed at some passing occurrence, must have obliterated from the minds of the unhappy men all perception of moral guilt, and thoroughly brutalized their feelings.

The argument, that such an amount of punishment was necessary to maintain the discipline, is quite untenable. In the first place, good discipline has not been maintained; and in the second, the history of Penal Establishments throughout the world, show clearly that Institutions distinguished for excess of punishment, are at the same time notorious for bad discipline. We are satisfied that the prisoners in the Kingston Penitentiary are quite as good a class of men to work upon as those of any prison in the Northern States. And while other similar Institutions have been made profitable to the public, and the discipline maintained with comparatively little punishment, this, with excessive punishment, has succeeded in no respect.

We are not satisfied, that corporal punishment can safely be prohibited in a Penitentiary; but we are decidedly of opinion, that its
exercise should be rare and marked, and only called out by the most
serious offences. Little good can be obtained by degrading a man in
his own estimation or in that of others. Convicts have the same feelings
as other men. Cases will undoubtedly arise, when it is necessary to
make a severe example, but frequent repetition will completely destroy
the effect.

We think the frightful amount of punishment which has been
inflicted in the Penitentiary, and the indiscriminate manner of its
application, admits of no apology.

    (D) Charge VIII, part 8 -- case of Alexis Lafleur -- against
            Warden Smith. [Lafleur aged 11 when committed 24 July
            1842; pardoned 26 July 1845; recommitted for four
            years 9 May 1846, aged 15. Complete and extensive list
            of punishments given and causes.]

The Warden brings evidence to show, that Lafleur is a wild
character, and there can be no doubt that his conduct has been that of
a troublesome bad boy, and that it may have been necessary to punish
him severely; but the offences for which he has been punished have been
generally, talking, laughing, and idling, and do not betoken depravity
so much as heedlessness; and it is very clear that if he was not
naturally bad, such a frightful amount of punishment must assuredly have
made him so. His punishment commences within three days after his
arrival, showing that no mild treatment was used towards the child
before the last resort was employed; and during his first committal,
he is flogged 38 times with the raw-hide, and 6 times with the cats.

It is horrifying to think of a child of 11 to 14 years of age,
being lacerated with the lash before 500 grown men; to say nothing of
the cruelty, the effect of such a scene, so often repeated, must have
been to the last degree brutalizing.

(E) Charge VIII, part 10 -- case of Peter Charboneau --
     against Warden Smith.

Edward Utting: 'A small boy, named Charboneau, was frequently
flogged with the cow-hide. He was a mere child. He should have had a
kind word, rather than punishment.'

Mr. Smith-guard: 'Charboneau's conduct was childish. He was
continually playing at tricks, as children would do.'

Thomas Fitzgerald: 'Recollects the boy Charboneau; he was a very
small boy; he was very frequently flogged with cow-hide. Witness
thinks he could have made more of him by advising him than by whipping.'

Francis Little: 'Charboneau is in witness's gang; his general
conduct is very bad; has had more difficulty with him than with five
other Convicts. He is in good health.'

Thomas Costen: 'Peter Charboneau is a very bad, troublesome little
boy; idle and talkative. Thinks reasoning would do no good with him;
has spoken to him frequently without effect; cannot tell his sentence.
As far as witness knows, he was never punished without a cause. There
is frequently more trouble with young Convicts than with grown men.'

The table shows that Charboneau's offences were of the most trifling
description -- such as were to be expected from a child of 10 or 11;
and that for these, he was stripped to the shirt, and publicly lashed
37 times in eight and a half months.

We can only regard this as a case of barbarity, disgraceful to
humanity.

(F) Charge VIII, part 11 -- Antoine Beauché -- against Warden
     Smith.

Head Keeper Costen: 'Recollects Antoine Beauché, the tailor
boy; he was continually breaking the rules of the Prison while here;
never saw him punished to his knowledge, without his offence being
entered in the book...Cannot say as he was punished with the cats; in
all the raw-hide punishments he received in witness's presence, the
lash was laid on lightly on account of his youth; has been stationed

in the dining-hall during punishment, ever since Antoine Beauché has
been in the Prison; his health was always very good; he left the
Prison; in excellent health; it was absolutely necessary to punish
him to keep him in proper order.'

Commissioners: 'The table shows that this child received the lash
within a week of his arrival, and that he had no fewer than 47 corporal
punishments in nine months, and all for offences of the most childish
character.

We regard this as another case of revolting inhumanity.'

   (G) <u>Charge VIII, part 13 -- case of Louis Beauché -- against
Warden Smith</u>.

Mr. Costen: 'Convict Louis Beauché was a very bad character; it
was necessary to punish him frequently to keep him in subjection.
Cannot say if he was ever punished with the cats; he was always very
healthy...'

Commissioners: 'This boy was flogged within three days of his
arrival, and got 39 punishments with the lash in the first eleven months
of his imprisonment. There have been three brothers of this name in
the Prison. One of them became insane in the Penitentiary, and is now
an inmate of the Beauport Lunatic Asylum. In the character of the
offences committed by all three of the brothers, a weakness of intellect
may perhaps be detected. In looking into such cases as this, one
cannot but feel that the merciful intervention of the late Government
was a most fortunate event.'

   (H) <u>Charge VIII, part 14 -- case of James Brown driven insane
against Warden Smith</u>.

The defense made by the Warden upon this charge is, that Brown is
not mad, but a violent, bad character, who deserved all the punishment
he got, and was the better of it.

Keeper Hermiston: 'Witness thinks that Brown has become worse
since punishment has ceased to be inflicted on him, his talk has become
much worse.' [ceased because doctor declared him to be insane]

Commissioners: 'Mr. Kirkpatrick has well described him as

'naturally a violent obstinate man, of low intellect"; a man without
sufficient judgment to carry him through the world. To subject a man
of this disposition to the cruel punishments which have been incessantly
inflicted on him for over eight years, is the direct way to drive him
mad....

The tables show that Brown was ordered 1002 lashes of the cats,
and 216 of the raw-hide; but 36 lashes of the cats having been stopped
by the Surgeon, the whole number of lashes inflicted on him has been
1182. Thirty-five times has this man been subject to the torture of
the cats.

We are well satisfied that whether a different treatment would
have been successful or not, if tried upon him, incessant and severe
punishment could only make him more reckless and stupid than before,
and we cannot doubt, that the treatment which he has received in the
Prison has greatly aggravated his pre-disposition to insanity.'

      (I)   Charge VIII, part 15 -- driving John Donovan insane
            -- against Warden Smith.

Mr. Smith-guard: '...Shortly after Donovan came in he was very
outrageous; after he had been frequently flogged, witness observed
that he became more outrageous; he became stark mad.'

Commissioners: 'The punishment inflicted on him is frightful.
Seven floggings with the cats in a fortnight, and fourteen floggings in
four weeks with cats or raw-hides. It is very clear that if the man
was deranged when he arrived, or had any tendency towards it, that the
treatment he received was calculated to drive him into hopeless insanity....
This case strongly manifests the reckless and unfeeling manner in which
corporal punishment has been awarded in the Penitentiary.'

57. Second Report of the Commissioners Appointed to Investigate into
    the Conduct, Discipline, and Management of the Provincial Peni-
    tentiary [The Brown Report].

    Journals of the Legislative Assembly (1849), Appendix B.B.B.B.B.
    [not paginated]

        With sincere pleasure, we turn from the topics which occupy
our first report, to the far more agreeable subject of those improvements on our Penitentiary system which the increased light thrown, of
late years, on the interesting question of prison discipline throughout
the world, and the personal knowledge of the subject we have acquired,
may enable us to suggest for Your Excellency's consideration.

        The vast number of human beings annually committed to prison in
every civilized country, and the reflection that there they may receive
fresh lessons in vice or be led into the path of virtue -- that, after
a brief space, they are to be thrown back on their old habits, more
deeply versed than before in the mysteries of crime, or returned
to society with new feelings, industrious habits, and good resolutions
for the future -- must ever render the management of penal Institutions
a study of deep importance for the Statesman as well as the Philanthropist.

        The time has been when the Prison was regarded as a mere place of
punishment, when fear was deemed the only passion by which prisoners
could be swayed, and the law of terror the only rule of discipline;
when a discharged Convict, no matter what his crime, was shunned as
the leper, and driven by the cold, unpitying cruelty of his fellow-
beings to despair, too often sought revenge by plunging into the lowest
abyss of guilt. But the labours of the great and good men who have
devoted their lives to the cause of the out-cast of society, have not
been fruitless; public attention has been gradually awakened to the
errors of the prevailing systems of prison discipline, and great
ameliorations have been effected. The dungeon gave way to the well
regulated apartment -- healthful labour has replaced vicious idleness
-- and now the general aim is to find in what manner the security of
the public, the prevention of crime, and the reformation of the criminal
can be best obtained without the appearance of revenge. And when it is
considered that a large proportion of the inmates of prisons are the
victims of circumstances; that many are condemned for the first act of

crime, and many more for the act of a moment of passion or intemperance; and that the great majority of prisoners have been born and reared in ignorance of everything but vice -- how strong is the claim on a Christian people to see well that their prisons shall not become the moral tomb of those who enter them, but rather schools where the ignorant are enlightened and the repentant strengthened -- in which expiation for crime is not lost sight of, but the permanent moral reform of the Convict is the chief aim.

In Canada, while the history of our prisons does not furnish the tales of horror, which those of Europe have so often unfolded, little progress has been made towards introducing the ameliorations and improvements which the wisdom and philanthropy of other countries have tested and approved. The juvenile offender is yet confined with the hoary-headed evil-doer -- we have as yet no asylum by which the child of vice and ignorance may be stopped and rescued on his first entry upon the path of crime -- in our common gaols the erring youth and the hardened offender, the innocent and the guilty, those committed for trial and those actually convicted, are too often found herded together in one apartment. We have but one penal Institution of which the aim is reformation, and the little success which has as yet attended its operations, it has been our painful duty to disclose.

At a very early stage of our inquiries, we became convinced that the discipline and management of the Kingston Penitentiary were susceptible of much improvement; our attention was consequently earnestly turned towards the reformatory systems in operation in other countries, with a view to culling the best portions of each and adapting them to the condition and requirements of our own land. The subject opened up for our consideration numerous points of greater or less importance; and notwithstanding our access to many valuable works and reports on prison discipline, we found that our task could not be efficiently executed without personal inspection of some of the best penal institutions of the neighbouring States. We accordingly, despatched two members of the Commission, Messrs. Bristow and Brown, on 6th November, to fulfil this mission. They were absent until the 10th December, having in the interval, visited the Penitentiaries of seven States.

[account of the "Deputation to the United States": 5 pp.]

COUNTY GAOLS.

At every step of our proceedings we have felt keenly that the entire penal system of the Province demands a thorough reform; and that so long as our Common Gaol system remains as at present, no satisfactory moral results can be expected from the higher institution. The District Gaols are the nurseries of crime and vice, and ere the prisoner is transferred from them to the Penitentiary, he is too often thoroughly contaminated and hardened. Men do not sink at once into the depths of crime -- the descent is gradual and imperceptible -- and while considering how to reform the criminal, we have constantly felt how much more desirable it would be to prevent the crime, and how much more hopeful would be the labor of leading the young offender into a good course, and inspire him with better feelings, than to eradicate habits which have been the growth of years.

Though the scope of our instructions did not extend beyond the Penitentiary, we have felt that the success of that Institution depends so much upon the Common Gaol system, that it was our duty to call Your Excellency's attention to the evils arising from it; and in considering the improvement of the Penitentiary system, we could not avoid associating with it, to some extent, the reform of gaol discipline throughout the Province. We cannot refrain from suggesting to Your Excellency whether the discipline of all the County Gaols might not, with advantage, be placed under the control of Government Inspectors, from whom periodical reports of their condition would emanate.

JUVENILE OFFENDERS.

Of scarcely less urgency than the reform of the gaols, is the necessity of some immediate action on behalf of the youthful delinquent. It is distressing to think that no distinction is now made between the child who has strayed for the first time from the path of honesty, or who perhaps has never been taught the meaning of sin, and the hardened offender of mature years. All are consigned together to the unutterable contamination of the common gaol; and by the lessons there learnt, soon become inmates of the Penitentiary.

We recommend to Your Excellency the immediate erection of one or more Houses of Refuge for the reformation of juvenile delinquents.

164.

Such an establishment might be economically built on the Penitentiary
lot at Kingston, and might be governed by the same Inspectors; but
the expense of transporting children so great a distance from the
extreme points of the Province, seems to make it necessary that there
should be a House of Refuge for both divisions of the Province; one
at Montreal or Quebec, and the other at Toronto or Hamilton.

We recommend that such House of Refuge consist of two departments:
one for children whose parents or guardians, by vagrancy or vicious
conduct, are unwilling or incapable of exercising proper care and
discipline over them; and for children whose parents and guardians
make complaint to the proper authority, that from the incorrigible
conduct of such children they are unable to control them; and the
other, for children who have been convicted of crime.

The control of the discipline and business affairs of such House
of Refuge might be advantageously placed in the hands of the Penitentiary Inspectors. The weekly visiting, the apprenticing of the
children, and the general carrying out of the philanthropic objects
of the Institution, might be vested in a large Board of Managers, to
be appointed by Government; or, as in the United States, in a society
of benevolent persons formed with this view.

All Criminal Courts of the Province might be empowered to commit
children to the House of Refuge; and any two Justices of the Peace
or City Magistrates, on a case being shown.

The managers of the institution should have the control of all
children so committed during their minority; and they should be
empowered to place them at such employments, and cause them to be
instructed in such branches of useful knowledge, as may be suited to
their years and capacities. They should also have power to
indenture the children as apprentices to such persons, and to learn
such trades, or other employments, as in their estimation will be most
conducive to their reformation and amendment, and will tend to
the future benefit and advantage of the children. During the continuation of his apprenticeship, the youth to remain still under the
control of the managers, and in case of irregular conduct, the

managers to have the power of bringing him back to the House of Refuge.
The children, in the two departments, to be kept strictly apart, but
the system to be the same, namely a combination of education, labor,
and healthful exercise.

––––––––––

THE PENITENTIARY SYSTEM.

The results to be drawn from all we have seen and read, and the
suggestions for the improvement of the Provincial Penitentiary, to be
offered for Your Excellency's consideration, have engaged our earnest
attention; and we have arrived unanimously at the conclusion to
recommend the combination of the two systems, the Separate and the
Congregate, in the future management of the Prison.

Were a new Penitentiary about to be erected, we might have been in
favour of a somewhat different plan; but with so costly and commodious
an establishment nearly completed, we are of opinion that the most
advisable course is to continue the Congregate system as the main
principle, and to engraft on it the ameliorating influences of
individual separation. We recommend to Your Excellency, the erection
of a sufficient number of cells to apply the Separate system to every
newly-arrived Convict; while so confined, the Convict to be furnished
with secular instruction and labour, and to earnestly dealt with by
the Chaplain and Warden. The length of this ordeal, we think, should
be left to the discretion of the Prison authorities, but should in no
case exceed six months; and the termination of it might in many cases
where mitigating circumstances existed, it is to be hoped, offer a
favourable opportunity of exercising the Royal Mercy with benefit to
society and to the Criminal.

Were it possible to judge correctly of each man's character,
classification would form the next step after the ordeal of separation
had been undergone. But this system, as far as it has yet been
attempted, has depended on so many elements -- as, for instance, the
nature of the Convict's crime, his previous character and position, his
conduct in Prison, and the prospect of his reformation, -- as to make
a correct classification, almost impossible, if not absolutely so. No
clear principle can be laid down to guide such a system; the whole

must depend on the judgment and discretion of the Warden. But
unsuccessful as the many experiments to carry out a complete plan of
this character have proved, we are not yet without some hope that it
might be partially introduced in amelioration of the Congregate system.

We recommend that the employments selected for the prisoners, be
as little diversified as possible, and that they may be such as can be
carried on within doors, and with the least needful communication
between the prisoners. It is exceedingly desirable that each gang
should occupy a separate apartment, and that the possibility of communication between them should be cut off; fortunately, the construction
of the Prison workshops will render this easily attainable. In rating
off the Convicts for the separate cells into gangs, in the hands of a
judicious Warden, we are persuaded experiments may be made in the way
of classification, which will prove highly advantageous; and while we
refrain from suggesting any rules for the regulation of the duty, we
would earnestly urge its high importance on the authorities of the
Penitentiary. Were it possible to keep every gang separate and secluded
from the rest of the prisoners, that worst evil of the Congregate
system, viz., that the Convict is known to so many Criminals on his
return to the world, would be partially avoided.

We recommend that besides employing the separate cells on the first
reception of the Convict, they be used as a means of discipline; not
as a frequent punishment, but in the case of continued refractory
conduct on the part of any Convict, to enable the Warden to deal with
him individually and endeavour to produce a change.

We recommend that fifty separate cells shall be the number at
first to be erected, and that they be built with all convenient speed.

We also recommend that apartments for the treatment of insane
Convicts, be erected within the walls. Heretofore the practice has
been, in such cases, to obtain the pardon of the patient and consign
him to the Provincial Lunatic Asylum until cured, when he was discharged from confinement.

It must be confessed that the success of any system of prison
discipline will be strongly affected by the treatment which the Convict
receives on his discharge from confinement. A Convict may leave his
cell penitent and determined to reform, but if he is met with harshness and refused employment, and his good resolutions treated with
scorn, despair will soon overtake him, poverty and the force of circumstances will too often drive him back to the haunts of crime.
Governments can do little to avert this snare from the path of the
reformed Criminal; the force of public opinion will alone effectually
remove the evil. Much has been done in the United States by prison
societies, who receive the penitent transgressor on his discharge, and
aid him and strengthen him in his struggle with the frowns of the
world; the tide of public sympathy has been, by their labours, turned
towards the helpless out-cast, and great good has undoubtedly been
effected. A more noble work could not engage the efforts of the Christian
or Philanthropist. We trust that such a society will, ere long, exist
in our own country, and that through the press and the lecture-room,
the subject of prison discipline may engage more attention from the
public than it has heretofore done.

The sum of money paid to the Convicts, on their discharge, is
altogether inadequate; and we respectfully recommend that the Warden
be empowered, in his discretion, to pay to each prisoner a sum not
less than £1, nor more than £5.

Our attention has been called to the great evils which arise from
Convicts being discharged from Prison in the depth of winter, often
far from home, without chance of employment, and with only a few
shillings in their possession. We suggest to Your Excellency, whether
the Judges might not, with benefit in many cases, sentence the
criminals to such terms as would bring their discharge at a more
auspicious season of the year.

Having thus submitted such a modification of the system of
discipline now in operation at the Provincial Penitentiary, as we
believe would conduce to its success as a Reformatory Institution, we
proceed to lay before Your Excellency the conclusions to which we
have arrived, after much anxious deliberation, as to the best mode of

managing its affairs, so as to "secure the confidence of the public,
and to increase its efficiency and utility."

The task of governing well such an Institution as the Kingston
Penitentiary, is evidently one of no ordinary difficulty. It is true
that so far as mere bodily coercion is concerned, the security is ample.
The walls of the Prison Buildings are of massive thickness; locks and
bolts and bars are there in profusion; the outer enclosure is so high
as to defy escalade, and in short effectual precautions have been
adopted to baffle any attempt at escape from within its precincts

Whatever other objections may be offered to the plan on which this
edifice has been erected, so far as regards the safe-keeping of the
prisoners it is unobjectionable.

Our former Report has abundantly shown that, as in the
construction of the Prison, in its internal economy and management,
the idea of physical force alone has been kept in view; whilst the
milder, but it is to be hoped the not less powerful influence of moral
suasion, has been altogether lost sight of. Here indeed the Penitentiary
system has been presented in its sternest aspect, and if the cat-o-
nine tails, the raw-hide, the box, the solitary cell, deprivation of
food, or of the light of heaven, could ever have deterred the criminal
from again preying on society, or violating its laws, here, at all
events, the salutary effect would have been produced; but we cannot
say that the experiment has proved successful, or that the torture
which the inmates endured within the walls of the Penitentiary, have
rendered their returns to it a matter of less frequent occurrence
than in similar Institutions, where a milder influence has prevailed.
Have the frequency and severity of punishment conduced even to the maintenance of the discipline of the Prison? The tables which we furnished
under this head in our former report clearly show, that the only effect
has been to render callous and to harden the offenders, and that each
addition to the weight of punishment has increased the number of
infractions of the Prison rules.

The history of the principal Penitentiaries in the United States,
conducted on the Congregate System, tell a similar tale of harshness

and cruelty, producing the very evils and disorders they are intended
to prevent.
[section of the duties of the warden, the inspectors and the prison
officers, 3 pp.]

MEANS OF MORAL REFORMATION.

Having thus particularized the duties of the several Officers under
the system which we recommend to Your Excellency's consideration, we
proceed to offer a few remarks on some points intimately connected with
the discipline and management of the Prison. And, as of first
importance, we earnestly recommend that the means of moral, religious
and secular instruction, shall occupy much greater prominence than they
at present do in our own or any of the American Penitentiaries. The
more deeply the subject is examined, the more forcibly is the truth
pressed home to our conviction, that ignorance is the parent of crime.
We conceive that the pecuniary interests of the Penitentiary should, in
no manner stand in the way of the reformation of the criminal; and
that, desirable as economy is, it is a sad mistake to sacrifice for
that consideration, all the higher objects of such an Institution. We
trust the Inspectors may be clothed with ample power to place the means
of secular and religious instruction on the best footing.

A feature in the Provincial Penitentiary which distinguishes it
from most others with which we are acquainted, is the admixture of
Convicts belonging to so many religious persuasions. The present law
provides a Chaplain to attend to the spiritual wants of the Convicts,
and makes no stipulation as to the particular Church to which he shall
appertain; but it is to be inferred that he is intended to be a Protestant, since further express provision is made for that large proportion of the Convicts confined in the Provincial Penitentiary who
are Roman Catholics. The Roman Catholic Bishop of Kingston or his
Coadjutor, or the ecclesiastical person administering the diocese, is
authorized from time to time to direct the attendance of a Roman Catholic
Priest at the Penitentiary, for the purpose of performing Divine Service
according to the rules and ceremonies of that church, to the Convicts
of that faith. And it is further provided that it shall be lawful for
the Board of Inspectors to make rules and regulations for the
admission, at proper and convenient times, of the clergymen or ministers

of any denomination of Christians, for the religious instruction of
such Convicts as may belong to the same denomination as any such
clergyman respectively.
[account of the difficulties that have arisen in the past from such
religious divisions and how that might be avoided in the future.]

We are of opinion that common education should form a systematic
part of the moral discipline, and should occupy the whole time of at
least one teacher. The several gangs should be drafted off to school
in rotation, and each Convict should be in school at least one hour every
second day. We would not hesitate to carry instruction beyond the
ordinary studies of reading and writing, but the Inspectors would be .
guided in this by the success which they might find to attend their
labors. To the School-master should probably be assigned the duty of
taking charge and distributing, under the directions of the
Chaplains, the books forming the library of the Institution. Holding,
as we do, that ignorance is the most fruitful parent of crime, we would
recommend the cultivation as well of the intellectual as of the moral
faculties of the Convicts, and for that purpose that a small library,
carefully selected, consisting principally of religious books, but
in part of useful works of a general character, should be procured.

REWARDS AND PUNISHMENTS.

Much has been written in favor of a graduation in the severity of
the Penitentiary discipline, founded on the conduct of the Convict
during his confinement. It has been proposed as an incentive to good
behaviour, that a regular record of the conduct of each individual
should be kept, and the classification adopted in each case founded on
the observance or non-observance of the Prison regulations.
Exemplary obedience would thus purchase privileges denied to those
who either occasionally or frequently infringed them. Convicts mani-
festing a determination habitually to violate the rules, to be
subjected to a greater rigor than the ordinary discipline of the Prison
imposes. This would open a wide door to favoritism, and even should
the strictest impartiality be shown in the grading of the Convicts, it
would be difficult to make them believe that such was the case. Each
would consider himself entitled to a higher rank than that occupied by
him, and comparing with the natural bias in favor of himself, the

offence for which he was undergoing punishment, with that of others by
whom he was surrounded, would draw the conclusion that he was treated
with injustice. All Convicts should as far as possible be placed on
the footing of perfect equality; each should know what he has to expect,
and his rights and obligations should be strictly defined. If he break
the Prison rules, he should also have the quantum of punishment to which
he becomes subject. He should not witness the spectacle of offences
similar in enormity treated with different degrees of severity,
unless in cases of frequent repetition. One of the most important
lessons to be impressed on the Convict's mind, is the justice of his
sentence, and the impartiality with which it is carried into execution.
This inflexibility by no means implies harshness as a necessary adjunct;
on the contrary the rules of the Prison should be carried out in a mild
and humane spirit. In place of wantonly seeking to degrade the criminal
below his present position, every means should be taken to raise him
above it. Each attempt to elevate the individual will act favorably
on the general mass. The Convicts should, as much as possible, be
made to understand that it is not the discipline to which they are
subjected in the Penitentiary that degrades them, but that the crime
which they committed outside has degraded them to the Penitentiary.
[recommendation that there should be no shortening of sentences for
good behaviour]

We have already exposed the cruel and indiscriminate character of
the punishments formerly inflicted at the Provincial Penitentiary, and
we need hardly add that we altogether deprecate the continuance of
such harshness. It is conceded now, as an admitted principle in
prison discipline, that there is no occasion to govern solely by
terror, and in the best regulated Institutions the lash is seldom, if
ever, resorted to. Some of the substitutes for the whip are perhaps
more open to objection than the whip itself. The shower or the bolt
bath has been proved to be dangerous to bodily health, and has produced,
in some cases, fatal results. It is also most unequal, acting with much
greater severity on some constitutions than on others. Another substitute
adopted at present in some Congregate prisons, is the yoke, an iron
bar of 30 to 50 pounds weight, fastened on the chest, and to the
extremities of which, the arms are extended and the hands tied. This
appeared to us a punishment of a revolting character, little calculated

to produce any salutary effect. Confinement in a dark cellar on bread and water, is perhaps better adapted to subdue refractory spirits, but this also requires care in the application, least either the mind or body should sink under it. The box, another _succedaneum_ for corporal punishment, which was used to so fearful an extent in the Provincial Penitentiary, during the year 1847, we are convinced, is highly injurious to some constitutions, and we see no prospect of such reformatory effects likely to be produced by it, as to justify the experiment. With proper management, our conviction is, that the punishments in a Penitentiary may be few in number and mild in character. There are, however, a few characters in most prisons whom too much lenity only tends to make refractory, and who are only to be ruled by bodily fear. On such persons and for such offences as seriously involved the discipline of the prison, such as assaults on the officers, it will undoubtedly be a matter of necessity, sometimes, to inflict the severe punishment of the dark cell, or failing that, of the cat; but we conceive, that with proper management, the deprivation of comforts, and solitary confinement, and as little of these as possible, will be found efficient aids to kindness and reason for the maintenance of good discipline.

[how convicts could be best employed]

ADMISSION OF VISITORS.

The indiscriminate admission of visitors, for the purpose of indulging a prurient curiosity, we consider fraught with such evil, that we recommend its discontinuance. It is discordant with the intention of Penitentiary confinement, which is to separate, as far as possible, the Convict from all communication with the world without; it distracts his attention from his labor, and excites him to infringe the prison regulations, forbidding him from gazing at strangers; it is the means sometimes of bringing improper characters into the prison, and of enabling them to hold intercourse with the Convicts: and it affords opportunities of supplying surreptitiously forbidden articles, such as tobacco, to the Convicts. In the Provincial Penitentiary, about 2000 persons have been admitted annually; and one man has been kept almost constantly employed escorting them through the yard and premises. In most or all of the Penitentiaries in the United States, an admission fee is exacted, which amounts in some to fifteen hundred to

two thousand dollars annually; but no revenue can alleviate the disgust
which every feeling mind must experience at the exhibition of so many
fellow beings, as in a menagerie, to the brutal or idle gaze of
spectators. Such an outrage on decency, we consider as second only to
the abomination which formerly existed of working the Convicts in
chains on the public highways.

The only visitors whom we would permit to have the right of intercourse in any shape, or access to the prisoners, besides the officers
of the prison, the Inspectors, and the official visitors, are the
members of the Executive Government and the Legislature, and the Judges
of the Court of Queen's Bench. Under peculiar circumstances the
Inspectors or the visitors might have the privilege of ordering the
admission of strangers, but this permission ought rarely to be granted
and not grow into a practice.

[recommendation that there be added to the penitentiary a "prison for
females", chapels for both Protestant and Catholic services, a school
room and water-works.]

We have thus gone through the various questions involved in the
inquiry entrusted to us by Your Excellency; and set forth the
improvements in the Management and Discipline of the Penitentiary,
necessary, in our opinion, for the better administration of the
institution, and for the physical and moral well-being of the Convicts.
In our investigations we have spared no labour to arrive at the truth
on every point, and our conclusions are the result of anxious
deliberation. The time occupied has far exceeded our expectations; but,
from the difficulties in our way, we feel that justice could not have
been done to all parties, and the subject satisfactorily treated, by
a shorter process. And if the result of our labours shall be to
replace the loose morality and the open mal-practices which have heretofore prevailed in the Penitentiary, by a high tone of moral feeling;
if a system of discipline, harsh, cruel, and degrading, can be made to
give way to one, firm, equable, mild and humanizing; if some success
shall be hereafter attained in the work of reformation; the time we
have devoted to the inquiry will not have been spent in vain. We are

well satisfied that if the spirit of our recommendations is promptly
carried out, all of these desirable results will be attained, and a
large pecuniary saving, annually effected.

In all our proceedings and recommendations, we have endeavoured
to keep steadily before us, that the great object of all penal
Institutions, is the prevention of crime; and it has ever appeared
to us that there are four great aims which a sound penal system
should ever keep in view, viz. -- to rescue the child of ignorance and
vice from the almost certain destruction to which he hastens; to
guard from contamination the venial offender, committed, before or
after conviction, for a brief space to the common Gaol; to implant
religious and moral principles and industrious habits on the inmate of
the Penitentiary; and to strengthen and encourage him in his struggles
with the world when he is discharged from confinement.

The results of all our researches has been, to impress us with the
wisdom and truthfulness of the declaration so early made in that British
Act of Parliament, which stands as an unperishable monument to the
philanthropic labours of Howard, that the true principles of a prison
system ought to be: -- "To seclude the prisoners from their former
associates; to separate those of whom hopes might be entertained from
those who are desperate; to teach them useful trades; to give them
religious instruction; and to provide them with a recommendation to
the world and the means of obtaining an honest livelihood, after the
expiration of their term of punishment."

All which is respectfully submitted,

ADAM FERGUSSON,

N. AMIOT,

E. CARTWRIGHT THOMAS,

W. BRISTOW,

GEO. BROWN,

Commissioners.

Montreal, 16th April, 1849.